The Secrets of Icarian Cuisine for Longevity

Chr. Boura-Stefanadi

The Secrets of Icarian Cuisine for Longevity

THE SECRETS OF ICARIAN CUISINE FOR LONGEVITY

ISBN: 978-960-489-098-9

PMP (Paschalidis Medical Publications, Ltd.).
14th, Tetrapoleos str., Athens, 115 27, Greece
Tel.: 003-210-7789125, 003-210-7793012, Fax: 003-210-7759421,
e-mail: orders: paschalidis@inbooks.gr
© information: gp@inbooks.gr, cp@inbooks.gr

Preface

It is common knowledge that people were always adjusting their dietary habits according to the products available into their environment. Nature provides the guidance to survival and paying the due respect to mother earth constitutes a contributing factor to health and longevity. The inhabitants of the island of Ikaria serve as a convincing example of the aforesaid notion since despite the fact that they do not possess any specialized knowledge nor they put excessive effort, they manage to live many more years while minimizing the possibility to suffer by cancer or any cardiovascular diseases. "I AM WHAT I EAT. MY FOOD IS MY MEDICINE", used to say the father of Medical Science Hippocrates.

People of Ikaria, as they lived isolated without being able to use transportation facilities, they had to tame the earth and the surrounding sea into order to survive. Mountainous Ikaria with the almost nonexistent plains and the steep slopes had to feed her children. Thus, the slopes became small terraces supported by dry walls, filled with fresh ground earth and dung, planted with trees that bear fruit as well as with fresh vegetables and herbs.

Free range goats were roaming the mountains (they are called raska) and the natives were keeping into their houses pigs, few goats, fewer chicken and even fewer cows.

The villages of the coast considered as their main source of nourishment the sea that is all kinds of fish and seafood which, because of the lack of road tracks, very rarely could reach to the mountainous villages.

People of Ikaria used all productive ways of developing anything that nature offered: They developed the cultivation of vine trees and they started producing wine (pramnios wine).

The variety of wild bushes bearing flowers with exquisite smell provided the opportunity to produce the finest honey which possesses all antibacterial

properties while it offers an important protection shield from cancer. This fine honey, the antioxidant properties possessing petimezi[1] – made by the must of grapes – as well as the honey made by carobs, were used as sweeteners. The diet of Ikarians was further enriched with dairy products, the fresh cheese kathoura or the salty myzithra, touloumotyri, some butter, yoghourt and fresh goats' milk.

Mountain offerings completed their healthy diet: herbs for the preparation of beverages and food, fliskouna[2], melissohorto[3], chamomile, oregano, thyme, wild greens, zohi[4], myronia[5], kafkalithres[6], galatsides[7], asparagus, bulbs, amanitas (mushrooms). Their table was further replenished by the wild fauna of the mountain: karivolous (snails), rabbits, partridges, thrushes, etc.

Through hard work and with the use of nature's gifts which seemed less than what they really were because of the needs of the usually numerous Ikarian families, the resourceful housewives had found the ways to fill their pots every day, to keep the fire of the stove burning and to maintain their household cattle.

Thus, with everyday dietary needs pressing and products (maxouli) varying to quantities or lacking due to season changes, the shifty Ikarian housewives found the ways to conserve the offerings of nature, especially at the times where the production of the latter was into sufficient numbers, so they could cover the household's needs throughout the year. Nonetheless, the flora and the fauna of the mountains were always contributing to that.

The inhabitants of Ikaria, while they respected nature, they discovered green ecological ways to preserve their products (maxouli), through the use of the hot summer beams of the sun, of sea salt, of vinegar made by grape juice and of olive oil.

During the summer, they were drying fruits and vegetables (tsifia), raisins, kaisia (apricots), figs as well as nuts such as almonds and walnuts; they were preserving fish and seafood into salt, e.g. octopus, tsiros[8] etc. and they were keeping all these into their cellars.

During the winter, they were picking the olives, they produced olive oil and they were preparing delicious olives delicacies into numerous varieties: Kourmades, kolimpites, tsakistes, into vinegar etc. Moreover, they were preserving chunks of pork into salt, they were preparing sausages and the remaining fat served as the raw material for the production of butter called glina. And, to end with, they were keeping all winter vegetables and nodules such as bulbs or kolokasi[9] into cans.

---

[1] Thick grape – juice syrup.
[2] Herbs growing in Ikaria as well as in the rest of Greece, used for the preparation of hot beverages.
[3] Herbes growing in Ikaria, used for the preparation of hot beverages.
[4] Wild greens growing in Ikaria as well as in the rest of Greece.
[5] Wild aromatic greens growing in Ikaria as well as in the rest of Greece.
[6] Idem
[7] Wild greens growing in Ikaria as well as in the rest of Greece.
[8] Salted small baby fish dried in the sun.
[9] Nodule that looks like potato.

The provision of the aforementioned possibilities together with the pressure caused by everyday dietary needs created into this isolated for centuries island the fully flavored, rich into taste aromas, assuring long life expectancy Ikarian recipes. And still, these recipes stood the test of times even when enemies and friends crossed the Mediterranean sea and reached the island bringing their extraneous dietary habits. They managed to alter, but not radically, the routine of Ikarian housewives since the latter adopt the new ideas through small variations and additions.

Into the course of time, those travelers who crossed sea borders as well as those who migrated enabled the development of commerce and thus, new products came to the island. Technology brought to the Ikarian house all the necessary information, all the necessary stimulus about other dietary habits (not only Mediterranean) and some of them were quickly assimilated to their diet.

Still, according to scientific views throughout the world about the advantages of Mediterranean cuisine and more over about the wisdom of the long life assuring Ikarian cuisine should not abandon, nor forget the Ikarian dietary habits.

Thus, while keeping into mind that have to preserve even a part of Ikarian cuisine which constitutes a window built into the past through which the light of the future shines bright, as well as maintaining the belief that the housewife of Ikaria with the use of her own simple, still unsurpassable ways of choosing and preparing everyday' s meals offered the gift of Ikarian longevity, as a minimum token of respect to my roots, to all that I heard and tasted by my mother, my grandmother, the aunties and all the village women throughout these years, to all that trusted to me by Ikarian women and men alike, I decided to publish this acquired knowledge.

The secrets of "Ikarian cuisine for Longevity" constitutes the accumulation of original recipes, adapted to contemporary life.

Chr. Boura – Stefanadi
November 2009

This cook book is dedicated to the loving memory of my mother Athena, who initiated me into the secrets of the cuisine of her native Mediterranean island IKARIA.

It is also dedicated to my beloved children, Ellie and Isidoros.

The Ikarian Dietary Pyramid

1. Base of the pyramid: fresh vegetables and fruits, greens - herbs, dried vegetables and fruits
2. Paximadi *(a type of rusk)* made by barley - bread - legumes - dry nuts
3. Pasta - rice - cereals
4. Oil - olives - wine
5. Potatoes and sweet potatoes
6. Fresh fish or fish preserved into salt
7. Dairy products
8. Eggs
9. Sweets
10. Pork meet fresh or preserved into salt - fresh goat meat
11. Lamb - veal - chicken

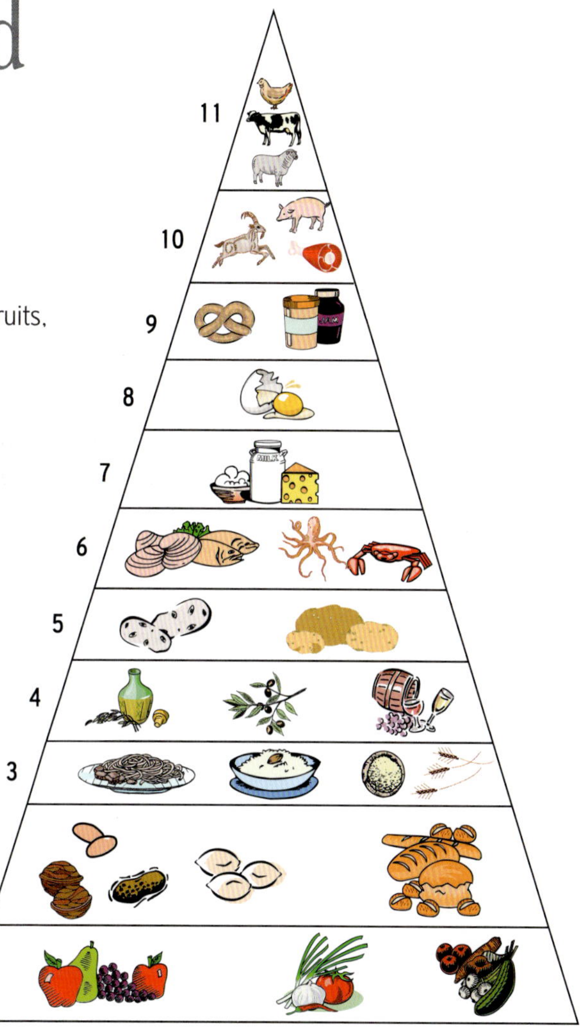

Contents

CONTENTS

CONTENTS

CONTENTS

The salad into Ikarian cuisine had not always been a complementary dish. Most of the times played the part of the main dish, accompanied with few olives or some cheese, whole meal bread and wine.

Salads

Cucumber salad with green almonds

INGREDIENTS

- 300 – 400 gr fresh almonds when they are still tender and green (not hard shelled)
- 4 finely chopped red peppers
- 1 finely chopped cucumber
- 2 medium sized onions, finely chopped
- ½ bunch finely chopped parsley
- 2 tbsp finely chopped spearmint
- ½ cup olive oil
- ¼ cup vinegar
- Salt
- Coarsely crushed black pepper

PREPARATION

1. Wash the fresh almonds, drain and put them into a salad bowl.

2. Clean, wash and finely chop the peppers, cucumber, onions, parsley and spearmint and add them to the salad bowl.

3. Season with salt and pepper. Whisk together the olive oil and vinegar and pour the dressing over the salad.

4. Mix the ingredients until they blend together, leave them for 5 – 10 minutes to marinate and serve.

Artichoke into vinegar with fennel

PREPARATION

1. Peel the outer leaves and discard the hairy choke of the artichokes. Keep the hearts and rub them with lemon to prevent discoloration.

2. Boil them into salted water until softened (not melted)

3. Drain, quarter and place them into the salad bowl.

4. Add the rest of the ingredients (except the olive oil and vinegar) and mix them until they blend together.

5. Whisk together the olive oil and vinegar and pour the dressing over the salad.

6. Mix all the ingredients so that they are all moistened by the dressing of olive oil and vinegar. Cover the salad bowl for half hour and serve.

INGREDIENTS

- 8 fresh medium sized artichokes
- ½ cup finely chopped pickled cucumbers
- 1 bunch fennel with its leaves cut into medium size
- 1 bunch finely chopped spearmint
- 4 finely chopped spring onions
- 1 cup black olives
- 1 cup finely chopped finokio
- ½ cup olive oil
- ¼ cup vinegar
- Salt
- Coarsely crashed black pepper
- 1 lemon for the artichokes

Wild dandelions (bitter)

INGREDIENTS

- 1 ½ kilo wild dandelions
- ½ cup olive oil
- ¼ cup vinegar
- Salt

PREPARATION

1. Remove the yellow leaves or hard stems from the dandelions.
2. Rinse any lumps of dirt and put them into a pan filled with plenty of salted water that is boiling.
3. Leave them to boil and when they are ready drain them.
4. Whisk together the olive oil and vinegar, pour the dressing over the dandelions and mix them to marinate.

Wild greens[1]

INGREDIENTS

- 1 ½ kilo various wild greens
- ½ cup olive oil
- Juice of 2 lemons
- Salt

PREPARATION

1. Clean the greens and rinse them thoroughly to remove any lumps of dirt.

2. Put them into salted boiling water and leave them to boil until they are done.

3. Drain and put them into a salad bowl and cut them with fork and knife.

4. Whisk together the olive oil and lemon, pour the dressing over the greens, mix and allow them to marinate for 30 minutes and then serve.

[1] They used to keep the water where the wild greens were boiled and drink it with lemon as beverage

Vive buds

INGREDIENTS

- 1 kilo vine buds
- ½ cup olive oil
- ¼ cup vinegar
- Salt

PREPARATION

1. Wash the buds and put them into salted boiling water.
2. Leave them to boil until they are done.
3. Drain them and peel their skin with a small knife.
4. Put the buds into a salad bowl, whisk together the olive oil and vinegar and pour the dressing over them.
5. Leave them to marinate for 30 minutes and then serve.

Spring beans with zucchini

PREPARATION

1. Remove the strings of spring beans, cut them in two pieces and wash them.

2. Wash and cut the zucchini in three pieces.

3. Put the spring beans with the zucchini into salted boiling water and leave them to boil until they are done.

4. Drain and place them into a salad bowl.

5. Add the onions.

6. Whisk together the olive oil, vinegar, crushed garlic; pour the dressing over the salad.

7. Add the parsley, mix the salad so that all ingredients get marinated and cover the salad bowl for 30 minutes before serve.

INGREDIENTS

- 1 kilo spring beans cleaned by their strings and cut into three pieces
- ½ kilo of medium sized zucchini cut into three pieces
- 3-4 garlic cloves crushed
- 2 medium sized onions cut into small slices
- 3 tbsp finely chopped parsley
- ½ cup olive oil
- ¼ cup vinegar
- Salt
- Coarsely crushed black pepper

Buds of wild and cultivated greens

INGREDIENTS

- Buds from sweet potatoes, zucchini, fennel, a variety of wild greens (all together 1½ kilo)
- 4 thinly sliced onions
- ½ cup olive oil
- Juice of 1-2 lemons
- 1 cup olives kourmades (throubes[1])
- Salt

PREPARATION

1. Wash the greens and chop them to small pieces.

2. Put them into a salad bowl, add the olives and onion, season with salt and pour over them a dressing of whisked olive oil and vinegar, or boiled them in salted water until they are done, drained them and then put them in a salad bowl.

3. Pour over them a dressing of olive oil and lemon and serve.

[1] Salted, small black olives.

Vlita[1] with zucchini

INGREDIENTS

- 1 kilo vlita tender cut in medium sized pieces
- 4-5 zucchini cut into three
- ½ cup olive oil
- ¼ cup vinegar
- Salt

PREPARATION

1. Remove the yellow leaves as well as the hard stems from vlita and wash them.
2. Grate gently the skin of zucchini and wash them.
3. Put vlita into salted boiling water and leave them to boil for 15 – 20 minutes.
4. Add the zucchini on top of vlita to prevent them from breaking and leave them to boil until they are done.
5. Remove the zucchini with a slotted spoon, cut and put them to a plate.
6. Drain the vlita and put them into a salad bowl.
7. Whisk together the olive oil and vinegar, pour the dressing over vlita, mix them to get marinated, add the zucchini, cover them with the marinated vlita for 10 minutes and serve.

[1] Greens growing in Greek land.

Salad of bulbs

(vorvi)

INGREDIENTS

- 1 kilo bulbs
- 4 pieces finely chopped fresh garlic or 4-5 dried garlic cloves, grated
- ¼ cup vinegar
- ½ cup olive oil
- Salt

PREPARATION

1. Peel the skin of the bulbs and wash them.

2. Put the bulbs into boiling water for 5 minutes, drain and allow them to cool into cold water for one hour.

3. Boil water again and put them inside for 5 - 10 minutes and then drain them.

4. Put the bulbs into salted boiling water, leave them until they are done and drain them.

5. Put the bulbs into a salad bowl and add the garlic.

6. Whisk together the olive oil and vinegar and pour the dressing over the contents of the salad bowl .

7. Mix the ingredients until they blend together and leave then to marinate for one hour before serve them.

Vorvi (bulbs) and lentils into vinegar

INGREDIENTS

- 500 gr bulbs
- 300 gr lentils
- 1 bunch tender celery, finely chopped
- ½ bunch finely chopped parsley
- 2 medium sized onions, sliced
- 1 tbsp oregano
- ½ cup olive oil
- ¼ cup vinegar
- Salt
- Pepper

PREPARATION

1. Peel the skin of the bulbs, wash and boil them into plenty of salted water until it is easy to pierce them with a fork.
2. Drain and place them into cold water for about 2 hours into order to lose any bitterness in taste.
3. Drain well and put them into a salad bowl.
4. Wash the lentils and boil them into salted water until they are done.
5. Drain and add them to the salad bowl.
6. Clean and wash the celery, parsley and onions, cut and place them also into the salad bowl.
7. Whisk together the olive oil and vinegar, add the pepper and pour the dressing over the salad. Add the salt and the oregano and blend all the ingredients.
8. Leave them to marinate for 10 – 15 minutes and then serve.

Buds of bulbs salad

INGREDIENTS

- 1 ½ kilo bulbs' buds cut into thick chunks
- 1 cup olive oil
- Juice of 1-2 lemons
- Salt

PREPARATION

1. Wash and cut the buds and put them into salted boiling water.
2. Leave them to boil for 30 – 45 minutes, drain well and place them into a salad bowl.
3. Whisk together the olive oil and lemon juice, pour the dressing over the salad, mix the ingredients together, leave them to marinate for 10 – 15 minutes and then serve.

Galatsides

INGREDIENTS

- 1 ½ kilo galatsides cut into medium sized pieces
- ½ cup olive oil
- Juice of 1-2 lemons
- Salt

PREPARATION

1. Clean, wash and cut galatsides.
2. Put the galatsides into salted boiling water and leave them to boil until they are done.
3. Drain well and put them into a salad bowl.
4. Whisk together the olive oil and lemon juice and pour the dressing over galatsides.
5. Mix them into order to get moistened by the marinade and then serve.

Salad of glistrida[1]

INGREDIENTS

- 800 gr of glistrida cut into thick chunks
- 2 finely chopped red peppers
- 1 sliced cucumber
- 4 thinly sliced spring onions
- ½ cup finelly chopped dill-(amise)
- 1 tbsp caper
- ½ cup olive oil
- ¼ cup vinegar
- Salt

PREPARATION

1. Clean glistrida form any yellow leaves, wash and leave it to drain, then cut and put it into a salad bowl.

2. Clean, wash and chop the rest of the vegetables.

3. Add them to the salad bowl and season with salt.

4. Whisk together the olive oil and vinegar, pour the dressing over the salad and mix all the ingredients until they blend together.

5. Add the caper and serve.

[1] Wild greens growing in Ikaria.

Sweet pumpkin with potatoes

INGREDIENTS

- 1 kilo of sweet pumpkin, the marrow, cut into big cubes
- 500 gr of potatoes cut into big cubes
- ½ of dill or tender leaves of finely chopped fennel
- 3 tbsp finely chopped spearmint, fresh or dry
- 3 spring onions finely chopped
- 1 medium sized onion, finely chopped
- 1 cup olive oil
- Juice of 2 lemons
- Salt
- Coarsely crushed black pepper

PREPARATION

1. Peel the skin of the pumpkin, cut it into big cubes and boil it into salted water until it is ready (not melted, soft but firm). Drain well and put it into a salad bowl.

2. Boil the potatoes into salted water after having them washed and cleaned.

3. When the potatoes are done, cut them into big cubes and put them into the salad bowl that already contains the pumpkin.

4. Add the clean and washed spring onions, the onion, the dill and the spearmint.

5. Whisk together the olive oil, lemon juice and pepper and pour the dressing over the salad.

6. Mix together all ingredients and cover the salad into order to marinate for about 30 minutes before serve.

Zohi[1]

INGREDIENTS

- 1 ½ kilo of zohi, halved
- 1 cup olive oil
- Juice of 2 lemons
- Salt
- Pepper

[1] Zohi, wild greens.

PREPARATION

1. Clean, cut and wash the zohi.
2. Put the zohi into plenty of salted boiling water, and boil them until they are done.
3. Drain all the remaining water and put them into a salad bowl.
4. Cut the zohi with knife and fork, whisk together the olive oil, lemon and pepper.
5. Pour the dressing over zohi, leave them to marinate for 15 minutes and then serve.

Summer salad

INGREDIENTS

- 1 kilo of sliced tomatoes
- 250gr small chunks of kathoura cheese
- 2 medium sized onions cut into slices
- 3 finely chopped green peppers
- 4 barley rusks crumbled into small pieces
- 1 heaped tbsp oregano
- ½ cup olive oil
- Salt

PREPARATION

1. Wash the vegetables, cut and put them into a salad bowl.

2. Add the rest of the ingredients, mix them in order to blend together and then serve.

Kafkalithres[1] - dandelions - wild leek

INGREDIENTS

- 1 kilo kafkalithres, wild sweet dandelions
- 3 tender spring onions, finely chopped
- 4 tender wild leeks, or finely chopped leeks
- Juice of 2 lemons
- ½ cup olive oil
- Salt
- Pepper

[1] Kafkalithres:

PREPARATION

1. Clean and wash all the vegetables.
2. Put kafkalithres and dandelions into salted boiling water.
3. Leave them to boil until they are done, drain all remaining water and place them in a salad bowl.
4. Cut the boiled greens into small bites using knife and fork.
5. Add the spring onions, leeks and season with pepper.
6. Whisk together the olive oil and lemon juice and pour the dressing over the salad, mix all the ingredients in order to blend together and marinate and then serve.

Kolokasi[1] with onion

PREPARATION

1. Peel the skin of kolokasi, wash, cut into medium sized chunks and boil it into salted water until it is easy to pierce it with a fork.

2. Drain all the water, wash it with cold water, cut it into small pieces and put it in the salad bowl.

3. Clean the onion, spring onions and parsley, chop them finely and put them to the salad bowl.

4. Whisk together the olive oil and lemon juice, add the pepper and pour the dressing over the salad.

5. Mix the salad in order to marinate and before serve it leave it covered for 15 – 20 minutes.

INGREDIENTS

- 1 kilo kolokasi roots cut into medium sized chunks
- 2 medium sized onions, finely chopped
- 3 finely chopped spring onions (only their green part)
- ½ cup olive oil
- Juice of 2 lemons
- 2 tbsp finely chopped parsley
- 2 tbsp finely chopped spearmint
- Salt
- Pepper

[1] Kolokasi: wild potato.

Kolokasi with red herring

INGREDIENTS

- 700-1000 gr kolokasi cut into medium sized pieces
- 1 red herring bearing eggs cut into small pieces, almost melted
- 5 finely chopped spring onions or 1 finely chopped big dried onion
- 1 bunch finely chopped dill
- 1 cup olive oil
- Juice of 2 lemons
- Pepper

PREPARATION

1. Peel the skin of kolokasi, wash and cut into medium sized pieces and boil it in water until softened.

2. Drain and put it in a salad bowl.

3. Add the spring onions and dill, as well as the red herring after cutting it into pieces with its skin peeled and its bones removed. Whisk the olive oil and lemon juice and pour the dressing over the salad.

4. Season with pepper, mix the ingredients in order to blend together and leave the salad to marinate for half an hour.

Zucchini flowers with sweet potato and peppers

INGREDIENTS

- 1 kilo zucchini flowers and tender leaves cut into medium sized pieces
- ½ kilo sweet potatoes cut into medium sized dices
- 2 finely chopped red peppers
- 4 finely chopped spring onions
- 2 tbsp finely chopped spearmint
- 2 tbsp finely chopped parsley
- Juice of 2 lemons
- ½ cup olive oil
- Salt
- Pepper

PREPARATION

1. Wash the zucchini flowers and their leaves, clean all lumps of dirt from the sweet potatoes and put them all into salted boiling water.

2. Leave them to boil until can pierce the sweet potatoes with a fork.

3. Drain cut and put them into a salad bowl.

4. Peel the skin of sweet potatoes, cut and add them to the salad bowl.

5. Remove the stems and discard the seeds of the pepper, cut the roots and peel the skin of spring onions wash, cut and add them to the salad bowl.

6. Add the spearmint and parsley, whisk together the olive-oil, lemon juice and pepper and pour the dressing over the salad. Mix all ingredients in order to marinate and leave the salad covered for 10 minutes just before serve.

Broad beans with fennel root

INGREDIENTS

- 500 gr seeds of broad beans
- 300 gr finely chopped fennel root
- 4 tender leeks, finely chopped, only the white part
- ½ bunch finely chopped parsley
- 2 medium sized onions finely chopped
- 2 tbsp finely chopped spearmint
- Juice of two lemons
- ½ cup olive oil
- Salt
- Pepper

PREPARATION

1. Remove the seeds from the broad beans, cut their small eye and place them into a salad bowl.

2. Clean the fennel root, leeks, onions, parsley, wash, chop finely and add them to the salad bowl.

3. Season with salt, pepper and spearmint.

4. Whisk together the olive oil and lemon juice, pour the dressing over the salad and leave the ingredients to marinate for 15 - 20 minutes just before serve.

Salad of broad beans and greens

INGREDIENTS

- 300 gr seeds of broad beans
- ½ kilo finely chopped various aromatic greens (mironia, kafkalithres)
- 1 bunch finely chopped rocket
- 4 thinly sliced spring onions
- ½ bunch finely chopped parsley
- ½ bunch finely chopped dill
- 1 cup olive oil
- ¼ cup vinegar
- Salt
- Pepper

PREPARATION

1. Remove the seeds of the broad beans, wash them and cut their small eye. Place them into a salad bowl.

2. Clean, cut the greens, parsley, dill, rocket, spring onions and add them to the broad beans.

3. Season with salt, whisk together the olive oil and vinegar and pour the dressing over the salad.

4. Add the pepper, mix until all ingredients in order to blend together and leave the salad to marinate for 15 minutes just before serve.

Broad beans buds with chickpeas

INGREDIENTS

- 300 gr chickpeas without the skin
- 700 gr finely chopped broad beans buds
- 4 finely chopped spring onions (even the green part)
- ½ bunch finely chopped fennel or dill
- 3 tbsp finely chopped spearmint
- 2 small or medium sized onions, cut into rounds
- 1 cup olive oil
- Juice of 2 lemons
- Salt
- Pepper

PREPARATION

1. Wash the chickpeas and soak them into water for 8 – 10 hours.
2. Boil the chickpeas until they are done (add the salt 15 minutes before remove them from the heat).
3. Drain and place them into a salad bowl.
4. Add the broad beans buds, spring onions, fennel, spearmint, onions, season with salt and pepper.
5. Whisk together the olive oil and lemon, pour the dressing over the salad, mix the ingredients in order to blend.
6. Leave the salad to marinate and then serve.

Cauliflower with celery

PREPARATION

1. Remove all the hard parts of the cauliflower, wash and cut it into small portions.

2. Wash and cut the celery.

3. Put the cauliflower and the celery into salted boiling water and leave them until they are done.

4. Drain and place them into a salad bowl.

5. Add the olives and pepper, whisk together the olive oil and lemon juice and pour the dressing over the salad.

6. Leave all ingredients to marinate for 10 – 15 minutes and then serve.

INGREDIENTS

- 1 kilo cauliflower cut into portions
- ½ kilo celery stalks cut into thick pieces
- ½ cup olives
- 1 cup olive oil
- Juice of 2 lemons
- Salt
- Pepper

Cauliflower with celery root and potatoes

INGREDIENTS

- Cauliflower (weighing about a kilo) cut into portions
- 1 celery root (weighing about half kilo) cut into big dices
- 3 - 4 bunches of celery cut into medium sized pieces
- 4 medium sized potatoes quartered
- 1 tbsp finely chopped spearmint
- ½ cup olive oil
- Juice of 2 lemons
- 2 medium sized onions, finely chopped
- 1 cup olives
- Salt

PREPARATION

1. Wash the cauliflower and remove all its leaves and hard stalks. (Still, keep the leaves). Cut it into portions.
2. Peel the outer skin of the celery root, wash and cut it.
3. Peel the skin of potatoes, cut and wash them.
4. Put all the above ingredients, as well as the leaves, in salted boiling water and when they are done drain well.
5. After draining place them into a salad bowl.
6. Add the olives, spearmint and onion.
7. Whisk together the olive oil and lemon juice and pour the dressing over the salad.
8. Mix all ingredients until the blend together and leave them covered for half hour just before serve.

Kritama[1] with peas and cucumber

INGREDIENTS

- 500 gr tender peas halved
- 300 gr kritama
- 1 cucumber diced
- 4 finely chopped spring onions
- 3 finely chopped radishes
- ½ bunch finely chopped parsley
- 2 tbsp finely chopped spearmint
- 1 cup olive oil
- Juice of 2 lemons
- Salt
- Pepper

[1] Wild greens growing in Ikaria.

PREPARATION

1. Put the peas into salted water in order to boil and when they are done, drain and place them in a salad bowl.

2. Boil the kritama into salted boiling water for 5 minutes, drain and add them to the salad bowl.

3. Add the rest of the ingredients, washed and cut (cucumber, spring onions, radishes, parsley, spearmint).

4. Whisk together the olive oil and lemon juice, pour the dressing over the salad, season with salt, pepper and mix all ingredients until they blend together.

5. Leave the salad to marinate for 10 minutes and then serve.

Kritama with potatoes and tomatoes

INGREDIENTS

- 300 gr kritama
- 500 gr potatoes cut in medium size cubes
- 4 medium size tomatoes cut in medium size cubes
- 2 medium size onions cut in slices
- 1 bunch of tender celery sprigs
- Juice of 2 lemons
- 1 hip tbsp oregano
- ½ cup olives kourmades (throubes)
- 1 cup olive oil
- Salt
- Pepper

PREPARATION

1. Thoroughly wash the potatoes to remove soil and boil them in salted water until done.
2. Peel, cut and put them in a salad bowl.
3. Wash the kritama, boil for 5 minutes and add them in the salad bowl.
4. Clean, wash and chop the tomatoes, the onions and the celery and add them in the salad bowl.
5. Add the olives, the oregano, slightly salt (only the tomatoes) and then stir the olive oil with lemon juice and pepper and pour the mixture over the salad. Thoroughly stir to blend the ingredients.
6. Leave the salad to marinate for 10 minutes and then serve.

Cabbage salad

PREPARATION

1. Clean and wash the cabbage, onions, parsley, carrots; drain them well.

2. Cut and place them into a salad bowl.

3. Whisk together the olive oil, lemon juice and salt and pour the dressing over the salad.

4. Mix the vegetables in order to marinate and serve.

INGREDIENTS

- 1 small white cabbage, finely chopped
- 1 bunch finely chopped parsley
- 2 medium sized onions, finely chopped
- 3 carrots grated
- Juice of 1 big lemon
- ½ cup olive oil
- Salt

Loubini[1] with kritama and leeks

INGREDIENTS

- 300 gr loubini
- 500 gr kritama cut in thick pieces
- 1 bunch finely chopped parsley
- 4 crushed garlic cloves
- 2 medium sized onions, finely chopped
- 4 finely chopped tender leeks, only the white part
- 2 tbsp finely chopped spearmint
- ½ cup olive oil
- 4′O cup vi• negar

Salt

PREPARATION

1. Boil loubini in water until softened (not melted), drain and place them into plenty of salted water in order to lose any bitterness.
2. Drain and rinse them with cold water, leave to get completely dry and place them in a salad bowl.
3. Wash kritama and boil them for 5 minutes.
4. Drain well and add them to the salad bowl.
5. Add the onions, parsley, spearmint, leeks and season with salt.
6. Whisk together the olive oil, vinegar and crushed garlic, pour the dressing over the salad, mix the ingredients in order to blend together, leave the salad to marinate for 15 minutes and serve.

[1] *You can find loubini, even sweet ones, in health food stores. If you use in your recipes sweet loubini, there is no need to go through the process of extracting the bitterness.*

Loubini with pickles and lettuce

PREPARATION

1. Boil loubini in water until softened (not melted).

2. Drain and put them in salted water in order to lose any bitter taste, changing the salted water many times during 24 hours (In Ikaria, the method used in the villages situated at the coast in order to remove any traces of bitterness is washing them with sea water). Rinse with cold water and place them into a salad bowl.

3. Clean, wash and finely chop the lettuce and the onion and put them in the salad bowl together with loubini.

4. Add the pickles.

5. Whisk together the olive oil, vinegar and salt and pour the dressing over the salad.

6. Mix all ingredients in order to blend together, cover the salad bowl and leave all contents to marinate for half hour just before serve.

INGREDIENTS

- 2 finely chopped lettuces
- 200 gr sweet and not bitter loubini (in health food stores)
- 2 finely chopped red pickled peppers
- 2 medium sized onions finely chopped
- 4 finely chopped pickled eggplants
- 1 cup olive oil
- 2 tbsp vinegar
- Salt

Mushrooms with kafkalithres

INGREDIENTS

- 500 thinly sliced white mushrooms
- 4 finely chopped spring onions
- 1 bunch finely chopped fennel or parsley
- 2 finely chopped tender leeks, the white part
- 2 cups tender kafkalithres finely chopped
- 1 cup olive oil
- Juice of 2 lemons
- Salt
- Pepper

PREPARATION

1. Remove the stalks of the mushrooms, wash and leave them to drain, peel their skin, cut and put them into a salad bowl and pour over them the juice of one lemon.

2. Clean and wash the rest of the vegetables, leave them to drain, chop and add them to the salad bowl.

3. Season the salad with salt, whisk together the olive oil with the rest of the lemon juice, pepper and pour the dressing over the salad.

4. Mix all ingredients in order to blend together, leave them to marinate for 10 -15 minutes and serve.

Mushrooms with red herring and lettuce

INGREDIENTS

- 2 medium sized lettuces finely chopped
- 300 gr thinly sliced white mushrooms
- 1 red herring cut in small pieces (almost melted)
- 4 thinly sliced radishes
- ½ bunch finely chopped dill
- 4 – 5 finely chopped spring onions (even their green part)
- Juice of 2 lemons
- ½ cup olive oil
- Pepper

PREPARATION

1. Clean and wash the lettuces and mushrooms, leave them to drain, peel the skin of the mushrooms, chop and place them into a salad bowl.

2. Add the radishes, clean and chop as well as the dill and spring onions.

3. Peel the skin of the red herring, remove the bones and the head.

4. Cut the red herring into small pieces and add it to the salad bowl.

5. Whisk together the olive oil, lemon juice and pepper, pour the dressing over the salad.

6. Mix all ingredients in order to blend together, leave them to marinate for 5 minutes and serve.

Fennel (finokio) root with lettuce and red herring

INGREDIENTS

- 1 -2 fennel roots 300 – 400 gr, finely chopped
- 2 finely chopped lettuces
- 1 red herring bearing eggs cut into small pieces
- 4 finely chopped spring onions
- ½ bunch finely chopped parsley
- Juice of 2 lemons
- ½ cup olive oil
- Pepper

PREPARATION

1. Clean, wash and chop the fennel roots, lettuces, spring onions, parsley and place them in a salad bowl.

2. Peel the skin of the red herring, remove the bones and the head. Keep the flesh and the eggs.

3. Cut the flesh and the eggs of the red herring and add them to the salad bowl.

4. Whisk together the olive oil, lemon juice and pepper, pour the dressing over the salad and mix all ingredients until they blend together.

5. Leave the salad to marinate for 5 minutes and then serve.

Fennel (finokio) root with potatoes

INGREDIENTS

- 500 gr potatoes cut in medium sized dices
- 300 gr finely chopped fennel roots
- 2 finely chopped green peppers
- 2 finely chopped red peppers
- 4 finely chopped spring onions
- ½ bunch finely chopped parsley
- 1 tbsp oregano
- 1 cup olive oil
- 1 cup kourmades olives (throubes)
- Juice of 2 lemons
- Salt
- Coarsely crushed black pepper

PREPARATION

1. Wash the potatoes until all lumps of dirt are removed and boil them in salted water until they are done.

2. Peel the skin of potatoes, cut and place them into a salad bowl.

3. Wash and finely chop the rest of the vegetables and add them to the salad bowl.

4. Season with salt, pepper and oregano, add the olives, whisk together the olive oil and lemon juice, pour the dressing over the salad and mix all ingredients until they blend together.

5. Leave the salad to marinate for 15 minutes and then serve.

Lettuce salad

INGREDIENTS

- 2 lettuces cut in small pieces
- 4 green onions cut in thin slices
- 1 bunch finely chopped anise
- 4 tbsp vinegar
- ½ cup olive oil
- Salt

PREPARATION

1. Clean and wash the greenstuffs, leave to drain and chop them.
2. Put the greenstuffs in a salad bowl.
3. Stir in a bowl the olive oil with the vinegar and salt and pour the mixture over the salad.
4. Stir carefully and serve.

Black eyed beans with fennel (finokio)

PREPARATION

1. Wash the beans and half boil them in water. Get rid of the water and put the beans into salted boiling water leaving them until they are done.

2. Drain and place them in a salad bowl.

3. Clean and wash the onion, spring onions and fennel, chop and add them to the salad bowl.

4. Whisk together the olive oil, lemon juice, garlic, pepper and pour the dressing over the salad.

5. Cover the salad leaving all ingredients to marinate for 30 minutes and then serve.

INGREDIENTS

- 500 gr black eyed beans (dried)
- 300 gr finely chopped fennel, only the tender leaves
- 1 big onion, finely chopped
- 4 finely chopped spring onions
- 3 – 4 crushed garlic cloves
- ½ cup olive oil
- Juice of 2 lemons
- Salt
- Coarsely crushed black pepper

Beetroot salad

INGREDIENTS

- 1 ½ kilo beetroots (leaves and bulbs)
- 4-5 crushed garlic cloves
- 1 cup olive oil
- ¼ cup vinegar
- Salt

PREPARATION

1. Remove the roots and the yellow leaves from the beetroots, cut the bulbs and leaves, carve with a knife a deep line at the one side of the bulbs and cut the leaves into medium sized pieces.

2. Rinse any lumps of dirt and put them into salted boiling water leaving them until softened.

3. Drain all water, peel the skin of the bulbs, slice and place them in a salad bowl together with the leaves.

4. Whisk together the olive oil, vinegar and the crushed garlic and pour the dressing over the salad.

5. Mix all ingredients until they blend together, cover the salad bowl for half hour leaving the salad to marinate and then serve.

Boiled broccoli

PREPARATION

1. Remove the hard stalks and wash the broccoli, cut into portions and put it in salted boiling water together with the garlic cloves until softened.

2. Drain all water, put it in a salad bowl and add the onions.

3. Whisk together the olive oil and lemon juice, pour the dressing over the salad, mix all ingredients in order to marinate and then serve.

INGREDIENTS

- 1 ½ kilo broccoli cut into portions
- 4-5 garlic cloves
- 2 onions, sliced
- ½ cup olive oil
- Juice of 2 lemons
- Salt

Tomato with rocket and peppers

INGREDIENTS

- 500 gr rockets thickly chopped
- 4 sliced tomatoes
- 2 finely chopped green peppers
- 2 finely chopped red peppers
- ½ cup crumbs of kathoura or myzithra cheese
- 4 finely chopped spring onions or 2 medium sized dried onions
- ½ cup olive oil
- ¼ cup vinegar
- 1 tbsp oregano
- Salt
- Pepper

PREPARATION

1. Clean, wash and chop rocket and place it into a salad bowl.

2. Clean and wash the tomatoes, peppers, spring onions, chop them finely and add them to the salad bowl.

3. Sprinkle the cheese and oregano, season with salt and pepper.

4. Whisk together the olive oil and vinegar, pour the dressing over the salad, mix all ingredients until they blend together, leave them to marinate for 5 minutes and then serve.

Tomato salad with glistrida[1]

PREPARATION

1. Wash the vegetables, cut and place them into a salad bowl.

2. Add the olives, caper and salt.

3. Whisk together the olive oil and vinegar, pour the dressing over the vegetables and mix all the ingredients until they blend together.

4. Serve immediately.

INGREDIENTS

- 800 gr sliced tomatoes
- 300 gr glistrida cut into big pieces
- 1 sliced cucumber
- 1 cup olives
- 1 tbsp caper
- ½ cup olive oil
- ¼ cup vinegar
- 2 medium sized onions, sliced
- Salt

[1] Glistrida: wild greens

Tomato salad with rocket

INGREDIENTS

- 800 gr sliced tomatoes
- 1 bunch thickly chopped rocket
- 2 medium sized onions, sliced
- 1 medium sized onion cut into rounds
- ½ cup finely chopped dill
- 1 cup crumbles of fresh kathoura cheese
- ½ cup olives
- 1 tbsp pickled caper
- 1 heaped tbsp oregano
- 2 -3 tbsp vinegar
- ½ cup olive oil
- Salt
- Pepper

PREPARATION

1. Clean and wash all vegetables, leave to drain, cut and place them into a salad bowl.

2. Add the cheese, olives, caper, oregano and salt.

3. Whisk together the olive oil, vinegar and pepper and pour the dressing over the salad.

4. Mix all ingredients until they blend together and serve.

Ovries[1] with artichokes

INGREDIENTS

- 5 artichokes, only the heart, cut into slices
- 500-600 gr ovries, only the tender part
- ½ cup olive oil
- ¼ cup vinegar
- 1 lemon
- Salt

PREPARATION

1. Discard the outer leaves of the artichoke and rub the hearts with lemon to avoid discoloration.
2. Wash and clean ovries and remove the tough stems.
3. Put the artichokes and ovries into salted boiling water and leave them to boil for 15 – 20 minutes.
4. Drain the water, cut the artichokes and place them together with ovries into a salad bowl.
5. Whisk together the olive oil and vinegar, pour the dressing over the salad, mix and serve.

[1] Ovries: wild greens

Potatoes with fennel, mironia and red herring

INGREDIENTS

- 1 kilo potatoes cut into small pieces
- ½ kilo various wild aromatic greens (mironia, kafkalithres, galatsides, and fennel) finely chopped
- 1 red herring cut into very small pieces (almost melted)
- 4 – 5 finely chopped spring onions
- 1 cup olive oil
- Juice of one big lemon
- 1 tbsp oregano
- Pepper

PREPARATION

1. Wash the potatoes thoroughly to remove any lumps of dirt and boil them in water.
2. Peel the skin of potatoes, cut into small pieces and put them into a salad bowl.
3. Clean and wash the greens, chop finely and put them into the salad bowl with the potatoes.
4. Add the finely chopped spring onions and mix all ingredients until they blend together.
5. Remove the skin, the bones and the head of the red herring, chop the flesh into very small pieces (almost melt it) and put it into the salad bowl together with the other ingredients.
6. Whisk together the olive oil, lemon juice, oregano, pepper and pour the dressing over the salad.
7. Mix the salad, leave it to marinate for 30 minutes and then serve.

Potatosalad

INGREDIENTS

- 1 kilo small round potatoes
- 1 cucumber cut into rounds
- 2 medium sized tomatoes, sliced
- 2 red peppers cut into small pieces
- 3 spring onions cut into thin rounds
- ½ cup finely chopped dill
- ½ cup finely chopped fresh spearmint
- ½ cup olive oil
- ¼ cup vinegar
- Salt
- Pepper

PREPARATION

1. Wash the potatoes thoroughly to remove any lumps of dirt and put them into slightly salted water to boil.

2. Peel their skin and place them into a salad bowl.

3. Wash the rest of the vegetables, leave to drain, cut and add them to the salad bowl.

4. Whisk together the olive oil, vinegar and salt and pour the dressing over the salad.

5. Season with pepper, mix the ingredients in order to blend together and leave them covered for 15 minutes just before serve.

Potatosalad with glistrida

INGREDIENTS

- 4 big potatoes cut into small pieces
- 300 gr finely chopped glistrida
- 2 medium sized tomatoes cut into medium slices
- 4 medium sized zucchini cut into rounds
- 3 spring onions cut into rounds
- ½ bunch finely chopped fennel
- 1 tbsp oregano
- ½ cup olives
- 1 cup olive oil
- ½ cup vinegar
- Salt

PREPARATION

1. Wash the potatoes and zucchini and boil them into salted water until softened.

2. Peel the skin of the potatoes, cut and place them into a salad bowl.

3. Add the zucchini, tomatoes, glistrida, fennel, spring onions, olives and oregano and season them with little salt.

4. Whisk together the olive oil and vinegar, pour the dressing over the salad and mix all ingredients until they blend together.

5. Cover the salad bowl for half hour in order to leave the vegetables to marinate and then serve.

Peppers with glistrida and cucumber

PREPARATION

1. Clean and wash all vegetables.

2. Cut and place them into a salad bowl.

3. Season with salt, whisk together the olive oil, vinegar and pepper, pour the dressing over the salad and mix it until all ingredients blend together.

4. Leave it for 5 minutes to marinate and then serve.

INGREDIENTS

- 500 gr finely chopped glistrida
- 2 tomatoes medium size cut in thin slices
- 4 finely chopped red peppers
- 1 finely chopped cucumber
- ½ bunch finely chopped parsley
- 2 medium sized onions sliced
- ½ cup olive oil
- ¼ cup vinegar
- Salt

Chickpeas with aromatic greens

INGREDIENTS

- 300 gr peeled chickpeas
- 1 kilo various aromatic greens (mironia, kafkalithres)
- 1 bunch finely chopped fennel, the tender parts
- 4 fresh spring onions finely cut into rounds
- 1 cup olive oil
- Juice of 2 lemons
- Salt
- Pepper

PREPARATION

1. Put the chickpeas into a bowl filled with water in order to soak for about 8 – 10 hours.
2. Put them into a pan with water in order to boil until softened (not melted) and while they are boiling skim off any foam.
3. Drain the chickpeas and place them into a salad bowl.
4. Clean and wash the greens, cut into big pieces and put them into the salad bowl that contains the chickpeas.
5. Wash and clean the spring onions, fennel, chop and add them to the salad bowl.
6. Whisk together the olive oil with lemon juice and pour the dressing over the salad.
7. Season the salad with salt and pepper and mix all ingredients in order to blend together.
8. Cover the salad bowl for 30 minutes and then serve.

Rocket with fresh broad beans and spearmint

INGREDIENTS

- 500 gr seeds of fresh and tender broad beans
- 1 bunch thickly chopped rocket
- 3 finely chopped spring onions
- 3 tbsp finely chopped spearmint
- ½ bunch finely chopped parsley
- 1 tbsp caper
- Juice of 2 lemons
- ½ cup olive oil
- Salt
- Coarsely crushed black pepper

PREPARATION

1. Wash the broad bean seeds, leave to drain and put them into a salad bowl.

2. Wash the rocket, spring onions, parsley, spearmint, drain, cut and add them to the salad bowl.

3. Add the caper, season with salt, whisk together olive oil, lemon juice and pepper, pour the dressing over the salad and mix all ingredients until they blend together.

4. Leave the salad to marinate for 15 minutes and then serve.

Spinach with garlic and pickled peppers

INGREDIENTS

- 1 kilo spinach, the upper leaves, thickly cut
- 4 crushed garlic cloves
- 2 pieces fresh and tender garlic, finely chopped
- 2 pickled red peppers finely chopped
- 1 bunch finely chopped dill
- 1 cup olive oil
- ¼ cup vinegar
- Salt
- Pepper

PREPARATION

1. Wash and clean the vegetables, cut and put them into a salad bowl.

2. Season with salt, whisk together the olive oil, vinegar, crushed garlic, pepper and pour the dressing over the salad.

3. Mix all ingredients until they blend together, leave them for 10 minutes in order to marinate and then serve.

Asparagus salad

INGREDIENTS

- 1 kilo tender asparagus, halved
- Juice of 2 lemons
- 1 cup olive oil
- Salt
- Coarsely crushed white pepper

PREPARATION

1. Clean and cut the asparagus.
2. Put the asparagus into salted boiling water and leave them to boil until softened.
3. Drain the water and put them into a salad bowl.
4. Whisk together the olive oil and lemon juice and pour the dressing over the salad.
5. Season with pepper, mix and serve.

Stifno[1] with zucchini and potatoes

INGREDIENTS

- 800 gr tender stifno cut into big pieces
- 600 gr medium sized zucchini cut into medium sized rounds
- 2 medium sized potatoes cut into medium sized pieces
- 3 -4 crushed garlic cloves
- Juice of 1 ½ lemon
- 1 cup olive oil
- Salt
- 2 tbsp finely chopped spearmint

PREPARATION

1. Wash the vegetables and boil them into salted water until they are done.
2. Drain the water, peel the potatoes, cut and place them into a salad bowl.
3. Add the stifno and zucchini after cut them.
4. Whisk together the olive oil and lemon juice, add the crushed garlic, pour the dressing over the vegetables and mix until all ingredients blend together.
5. Cover the salad bowl vegetables to marina half hour.
6. Sprinkle the spearmint and serve.

[1] Wild greens growing in Ikaria.

Nettle salad

PREPARATION

1. Wash nettle

2. Put nettle into salted boiling water and leave them to boil until they are done.

3. Drain the water and put them into a salad bowl.

4. Whisk together the olive oil and lemon juice and pour the dressing over the salad.

5. Mix the salad in order to marinate and then serve.

INGREDIENTS

- 1 kilo tender nettle buds
- ½ cup olive oil
- Juice of 1 -2 lemons or vinegar
- Salt

Lentils with fennel (finokio) root

INGREDIENTS

- 300 gr lentils
- 700 gr fennel root, finely chopped
- 2 medium sized onions, finely chopped
- ½ bunch finely chopped parsley
- 3 tbsp spearmint
- 1 tbsp oregano
- 1 cup olive oil
- ¼ cup vinegar
- ½ cup kourmades olives (throubes)
- Salt
- Pepper

PREPARATION

1. Boil the lentils into salted water until they are done, drain all the water and put them into a salad bowl.

2. Remove the tough parts from the fennel roots, wash, cut and add them to the salad bowl.

3. Clean the onions, parsley, spearmint, wash and put them into the salad bowl.

4. Add the olives, a pinch of salt, pepper, oregano, whisk together the olive oil and vinegar and pour the dressing over the salad.

5. Mix the ingredients until they blend together and leave the salad to marinate for 15 minutes before serve.

Bean salad

INGREDIENTS

- 500 gr small bean seeds
- 4 – 5 finely chopped spring onions (even the green part)
- 2 finely chopped red peppers
- 1 finely chopped green pepper
- 2 tbsp finely chopped parsley
- 1 tbsp oregano
- 1 cup olive oil
- Juice of 2 lemons
- Salt
- Pepper

PREPARATION

1. Wash the beans and leave them to soak for 8 – 10 hours in plenty of water.

2. Drain all water and put them into a pan filled with water in order to boil until they are done. Season them with salt 15 minutes just before take them out of the pan.

3. Drain all remaining water and put them into a salad bowl.

4. Wash the spring onions, peppers, parsley, chop and add them to the salad bowl.

5. Add the oregano, pepper, whisk together the olive oil and lemon juice and pour the dressing over the salad.

6. Mix all ingredients until they blend together, leave them to marinate for 10 -1 5 minutes and then serve.

Fresh broad beans with fennel (finokio)

INGREDIENTS

- 1 kilo broad beans cut into medium sized pieces
- 1 bunch finely chopped fennel
- 4 – 5 finely chopped spring onions
- ½ cup olive oil
- 2 lemons (the juice)
- Salt
- Pepper

PREPARATION

1. Remove the side strings of the broad beans, cut and put them into salted boiling water until they are done.
2. Drain all water and place the broad beans into a salad bowl.
3. Clean and wash the fennel and the spring onions, chop finely and add them to the salad bowl.
4. Whisk together the olive oil, lemon juice and pepper, pour the dressing over the salad, mix and then serve.

Greek salad

PREPARATION

1. Wash and cut the vegetables.

2. Place them into a salad bowl, add the olives, oregano, salt.

3. Whisk together the olive oil and vinegar, pour the dressing over all the ingredients and mix them in order to blend together.

4. Serve immediately.

INGREDIENTS

- 4 sliced tomatoes
- 2 small and tender xilagoura[1] or finely chopped cucumbers
- 2 finely chopped red peppers
- 2 finely chopped green peppers
- 2 medium sized onions, sliced
- 1 cup olives
- ½ tbsp oregano
- ¼ cup olive oil
- 3 tbsp vinegar
- Salt

[1]Xilagoura: Kind of cucumber.

Omelettes

Artichoke omelette

INGREDIENTS

- 4 -5 artichokes, only their hearts, thinly sliced
- 2 grated carrots
- 4 finely chopped spring onions
- 2 tender leeks finely chopped
- 1/2 bunch finely chopped dill
- 1 cup finely chopped fennel root (finokio)
- 8 beaten eggs
- Olive oil
- Salt
- Coarsely crushed black pepper
- Cheese optionally

PREPARATION

1. Clean the artichokes, keep the hearts and cut them.

2. Place the artichokes into a frying pan with a little bit of water in order to soften.

3. When they are soft and the water has evaporated, add to the frying pan a little bit of olive oil, the spring onions, dill, leeks, fennel root, carrots in order to sauté them until softened.

4. Whisk together the eggs, pepper and little bit of salt and pour the mixture over the frying pan with the sautéed vegetables.

5. Reduce the heat and stir until the eggs are set and slightly golden.

Omelette with onion buds (karonous)

INGREDIENTS

- 500 gr finely chopped karonous (onion buds)
- 2 finely chopped red peppers
- ½ bunch finely chopped parsley
- 2 tbsp finely chopped spearmint
- 8 beaten eggs
- Olive oil
- Salt
- Coarsely crushed black pepper
- Cheese optionally

PREPARATION

1. Wash the karonous, peppers, parsley and spearmint, chop and place them into the frying pan with little bit of olive oil until sautéed and softened.

2. Whisk together the eggs, salt and pepper and put them into the frying pan with the sautéed ingredients.

3. Reduce the heat and stir until the eggs are set and slightly golden.

Omelette with manites (mushrooms)

PREPARATION

1. Place into a frying pan the mushrooms, spring onions, parsley, dill, carrots, spearmint, little bit of olive oil, stir and sauté them until softened.

2. Whisk together the eggs, salt and pepper and add them to the frying pan with the sautéed ingredients.

3. Reduce the heat and leave the bottom side of the omelet to fry until golden.

4. Turn over the omelette so that its bottom side becomes also golden or stir the eggs until set and serve.

INGREDIENTS

- 8 eggs
- 4 cups finely chopped mushrooms
- 2 finely chopped spring onions
- ½ bunch finely chopped parsley
- ½ bunch finely chopped dill
- 2 tbsp finely chopped spearmint
- 2 grated carrots
- Olive oil
- Salt
- Coarsely crushed black pepper
- Cheese optionally

Omelette with zucchini

INGREDIENTS

- 500 gr thinly sliced zucchini
- 6 finely chopped spring onions
- 1 cup finely chopped tomatoes
- 2 finely chopped leeks
- ½ bunch finely chopped parsley
- 2 – 3 tbsp finely chopped spearmint
- 8 beaten eggs
- Olive oil
- Salt
- Coarsely crushed black pepper and nutmeg
- Cheese optionally

PREPARATION

1. Fry the zucchini and place them into a colander to drain any olive oil left.

2. Keep a small amount of olive oil into the frying pan, add the spring onions, leeks, tomato, parsley, spearmint and sauté them until softened.

3. Whisk together the eggs, salt, pepper and nutmeg into a deep bowl and dip the zucchini into the mixture so that they are moistened on both sides.

4. Put the eggs and zucchini into the frying pan with the rest of the ingredients, lower the heat and stir until the eggs become set and slightly golden.

Omelette with zucchini flowers and potatoes

PREPARATION

1. Wash the zucchini flowers, leave them to drain all water and fry them with olive oil until they turn golden. Leave them into a colander to drain any olive oil left.

2. Clean, wash, cut, fry the potatoes with olive oil and place them into the colander with the zucchini flowers.

3. Keep little bit of olive oil into the frying pan, place it over the heat and add the onions, tomatoes, spearmint and parsley. Cook until all ingredients become sautéed.

4. In a small basin whisk the eggs, salt, pepper and nutmeg.

5. Add the zucchini flowers into the mixture so that they get moistened by it.

6. Layer into the frying pan all the sautéed ingredients and the potatoes, lower the heat and pour the eggs mixture with the zucchini flowers over them.

7. Stir until the eggs become set and slightly golden.

INGREDIENTS

- 12 – 15 halved zucchini flowers
- 2 medium sized onions finely chopped
- 2 thinly sliced potatoes
- 2 tbsp finely chopped spearmint
- 2 -3 tbsp finely chopped parsley
- 2 medium sized tomatoes finely chopped
- 8 beaten eggs
- Olive oil
- Salt
- Coarsely crushed black pepper and nutmeg
- Cheese optionally

Omelette with sausages – strapatsada

INGREDIENTS

- 400 gr sausages cut into rounds
- 4 finely chopped spring onions
- 2 finely chopped leeks
- ½ bunch finely chopped dill or fennel
- 2 finely chopped green peppers
- 2 -3 tbsp finely chopped spearmint
- 2 finely chopped tomatoes
- 8 beaten eggs
- Olive oil or butter
- Salt
- Coarsely crushed black pepper
- Cheese optionally

PREPARATION

1. Put little bit of olive oil into the frying pan, add the spring onions, dill, spearmint, peppers, leeks, tomatoes and sauté them until softened.

2. Add the sausages and mix them with the rest of the ingredients.

3. In a small basin whisk the eggs and little bit of salt as well as pepper and pour the mixture over the frying pan.

4. Reduce the heat and stir until the eggs become set and slightly golden.

Omelette with eggplant

PREPARATION

1. Place the eggplants into a frying pan with olive oil in order to fry them and when they are done put them into a colander to drain the excessive amounts of remaining olive oil.

2. Put little bit of olive oil, the carrots, parsley, onions, tomatoes and spearmint into a frying pan, mix all ingredients until they blend together and leave them to sauté and to strain all cooking juices.

3. Add the eggplants and mix together all ingredients.

4. Whisk the eggs, salt and pepper and also pour this mixture over the frying pan.

5. Lower the heat and stir until the eggs become set and slightly golden.

INGREDIENTS

- 2- 3 medium sized eggplants, diced
- ½ bunch finely chopped parsley
- 2 medium sized onions cut into small slices
- 2 grated carrots
- 2 big tomatoes finely chopped
- 2 tbsp finely chopped spearmint
- 8 beaten eggs
- Olive oil
- Salt
- Coarsely crushed black pepper
- Cheese optionally

Omelette with aromatic greens

INGREDIENTS

- 400 – 500 gr greens (mironia – kafkalithres)
- 1 big onion finely chopped
- 2 finely chopped leeks
- 2 grated carrots
- 2 medium sized tomatoes, finely chopped
- 2 tbsp finely chopped spearmint
- 8 beaten eggs
- Olive oil
- Salt
- Coarsely crushed black pepper
- Cheese optionally

PREPARATION

1. Clean, wash and chop the greens into medium sized pieces and place them into a large frying pan with little bit of olive oil and a small amount of water and saute them until softened.

2. Add the rest of the vegetables and the spearmint into the frying pan. mix and sauté all ingredients making sure that all cooking juices are strained.

3. Whisk together the eggs, salt and pepper and pour the mixture over the frying pan that contains the sautéed vegetables.

4. Reduce the heat and stir until the eggs become set and slightly golden brown.

Omelette with tomatoes

INGREDIENTS

- 8 beaten eggs
- 4 big tomatoes, finely chopped
- ½ bunch finely chopped parsley
- 2 finely chopped green peppers
- 1 big onion finely chopped
- 2 tbsp finely chopped spearmint
- Salt
- Pepper
- 1 tbsp fennel seeds
- Olive oil
- Cheese optionally

PREPARATION

1. Clean, wash and chop the vegetables and place them into a frying pan that contains ½ cup of olive oil.

2. Add the salt, fennel seeds, spearmint, pepper and fry all ingredients until softened and all cooking juices are strained.

3. Beat the eggs and add them to the frying pan.

4. Stir the mixture of eggs and vegetables until they become set and slightly golden.

Omelette with ovries[1]

PREPARATION

1. Clean the ovries, parsley, carrots, spring onions, leeks, wash, chop and leave them to drain all water.

2. Sprinkle little bit of olive oil into a frying pan, place it over the heat to get warm and add the spring onions, leeks, ovries, carrots and parsley, sauté them until softened (and not black).

3. Whisk together the eggs, salt, pepper, nutmeg and pour the mixture over the frying pan with the sautéed vegetables.

4. Lower the heat and stir until the eggs become set and slightly golden brown.

INGREDIENTS

- 500 gr ovries cut into medium sized pieces
- 4 finely chopped spring onions
- ½ finely chopped parsley
- 2 finely chopped leeks, only the white part
- 2 grated carrots
- 8 beaten eggs
- Olive oil
- Salt
- Coarsely crushed black pepper and nutmeg
- Cheese optionally

[1] Ovries: wild green buds.

Omelette with potatoes

INGREDIENTS

- 4 big potatoes cut into big dices
- 8 beaten eggs
- 1 cup olive oil or butter
- Salt
- Coarsely crushed black pepper
- Cheese optionally

PREPARATION

1. Clean, wash and cut the potatoes, put the olive oil or butter into a large frying pan. When the butter gets warm and starts melting, add the potatoes, cover the frying pan, reduce the heat and leave them to fry slowly until they are done.

2. Remove the potatoes from the frying pan and place them into a deep plate.

3. Whisk together the eggs, salt and pepper, pour the mixture over the plate with the potatoes and mix all ingredients together.

4. Place the frying pan containing little bit of olive oil over the heat, add the potatoes and eggs and leave them to fry until the omelet becomes set and slightly golden from one side.

5. Turn over the omelet and when it is done from both sides, serve immediately.

Omelette with asparagus

PREPARATION

1. Sprinkle little bit of olive oil into a frying pan and add the asparagus, onion, dill and small amount of water.

2. Sauté the ingredients until softened.

3. Whisk together the eggs and little bit of salt, little bit of pepper, nutmeg and pour the mixture over the frying pan with the sautéed vegetables.

4. Lower the heat and stir until the eggs become set and slightly golden.

INGREDIENTS

- 400 thickly chopped asparagus
- 1 big onion finely chopped
- ½ bunch finely chopped dill
- Olive oil
- Salt
- Coarsely crushed black pepper and nutmeg
- Cheese optionally

Rice | Vegetables
Legumes

Artichokes with peas

INGREDIENTS

- 8 artichokes, the hearts
- 500 gr fresh peas, (only the seeds)
- 4 potatoes, quartered
- 2 carrots cut into thin rounds
- 1 bunch finely chopped fennel
- 2 medium sized onions, finely chopped
- Juice of 2 lemons (little bit of juice for the artichokes)
- 2 tbsp flour
- 1 cup olive oil
- Salt
- Pepper

PREPARATION

1. Remove the tough outer leaves and the hairy choke of the artichokes, wash and rub them with a lemon to avoid discoloration.

2. Clean and wash the peas, potatoes, onions, fennel and carrots.

3. Put the olive oil into a large pan placed over low heat, add the onions, fennel, artichokes, peas, potatoes, carrots and stir in order to sauté them.

4. Half cover all ingredients with water, season with pepper and salt and leave them until they are done.

5. Make sure that 2 -3 glasses of stock are left in the pan by the end of cooking.

6. Remove the pan from the heat. Mix in a bowl the flour with little bit from the stock, some lemon juice and pour it over the contents of the pan.

7. Place the pan over low heat and bring just to the boil until the sauce becomes smooth. Serve.

Artichokes with fennel (finokio) roots

PREPARATION

1. Remove the tough outer leaves and the hairy choke of the artichokes, wash, rub them with lemon to avoid discoloration and place them into a pan.

2. Add the olive oil spring onions, fennel roots, parsley, carrots and potatoes, sauté them until softened and slightly golden.

3. Sprinkle the lemon juice, pepper and salt, half cover all vegetables with water, reduce the heat and cook until the food is done.

INGREDIENTS

- 8 halved artichokes (the hearts)
- 500 gr fennel roots cut into medium sized slices
- 5 – 6 finely chopped spring onions
- 4 potatoes, quartered
- 1 bunch finely chopped fennel
- Juice of 2 lemons
- 4 carrots cut into rounds
- 1 cup olive oil
- Salt
- Pepper

Artichokes and broad beans

INGREDIENTS

- 8 artichokes, only the hearts
- 500 gr fresh broad beans, very tender
- 4 – 5 finely chopped spring onions
- 1 bunch finely chopped dill or fennel
- 2 finely chopped carrots
- Juice of 2 lemons
- 1 cup olive oil
- 2 heaped tbsp corn – flour or flour
- Salt
- Coarsely crushed black pepper

PREPARATION

1. Remove the strings of the broad beans, wash and put them into boiling water for 5 – 6 minutes, drain and keep them aside.

2. Remove the tough outer leaves and the hairy choke of the artichokes, keep the hearts, wash, rub with lemon and place them into a pan that contains the olive oil.

3. Add the spring onions, dill, carrots and broad beans, sauté all vegetables until softened and until the onion becomes golden.

4. Half cover the contents of the pan with water, season with pepper and salt and leave the food to boil over low heat until 2 cups of stock are left in the pan.

5. Mix the corn flour with some stock and lemon juice, pour the mixture over the food, shake the pan to help the sauce cover all vegetables, bring the food just to the boil and remove it from the heat.

Wild greens and potatoes giahni[1]

PREPARATION

1. Clean, wash and chop the greens, potatoes, onion, parsley, fennel and place them into a pan with olive oil until softened.

2. Add the tomato, spring onions, pepper, all spice, salt and half cover them with water.

3. Leave them to boil over low heat until they are done.

INGREDIENTS

- 1 kilo sweet wild greens (zohi, galatsides, mironia) cut into medium sized pieces
- 500 gr potatoes
- 8 small onions (kokaria)
- 1 big onion finely chopped
- ½ bunch finely chopped parsley
- ½ finely chopped fennel
- 400 gr finely chopped tomatoes
- 1 cup olive oil
- Salt
- Pepper
- 5 – 6 all spice seeds

[1] Cooking method where all ingredients boil over low heat and, most of the times, in thick tomato sauce.

String beans giahni

INGREDIENTS

- 1 kilo string beans cut into medium sized pieces
- 1 bunch finely chopped parsley
- 1 big onion finely chopped
- 5 – 6 finely chopped garlic cloves
- 500 gr fresh ripe tomatoes, finely chopped
- 1 cup olive oil
- Salt
- Pepper

PREPARATION

1. Clean, wash and cut the beans.

2. Put the olive oil, onion, garlic, beans in a pan, sauté them until little bit softened.

3. Add the tomato and parsley, season with salt and pepper, half cover all ingredients with water, reduce the heat and leave them to boil until the beans are done and the sauce takes a smooth texture.

Fried chervil
(fern's buds)

INGREDIENTS

- 1 kilo chervil, the buds
- Flour for the coating
- Salt
- Frying olive oil

PREPARATION

1. Wash the buds and drain them.

2. Put the flour, salt and water (as much as needed) in a basin in order to make a thick pulp.

3. Place the frying pan with the olive oil over the heat, dip the buds into the pulp and put them into the hot olive oil until they get golden.

4. Remove them from the frying pan with a slotted spoon and serve them hot.

Stuffed zucchini

INGREDIENTS

- 8 big zucchini, halved
- 16 thin rounds of carrots to be used as caps
- 16 tbsp carolina rice
- 2 big onions, grated
- ½ bunch finely chopped parsley
- ½ finely chopped fennel or dill
- 2 medium sized carrots, grated
- 2 tbsp finely chopped spearmint
- 3 tbsp flour
- ½ cup olive oil for the stuffing
- ½ cup olive oil for the pan
- 3 cups stock from the food
- Juice of 2 lemons
- Salt
- Coarsely crushed black pepper

PREPARATION

1. Remove the stems from the zucchini, wash and cut them in half, and remove the flesh using a special utensil or a tea spoon.

2. Place the zucchini into a large pan with their open end facing upwards and put into a frying pan their flesh after being finely chopped.

3. Add in the frying pan the rice, onions, dill, parsley, spearmint, carrots, olive oil, season with salt and pepper and mix all ingredients until they blend together.

4. Sauté them over low heat until the vegetables get softened, remove them from the heat and fill the cavities of the zucchini with the stuffing.

5. Cover the zucchini with the rounds of carrots, half cover the food with water, add ½ cup of olive oil, little bit of salt, little bit of pepper and leave them over low heat until they are done.

6. Whisk together the lemon juice, flour and 3 cups of stock form the pan, pour over the zucchini, leave them to come just to the boil and until the sauce becomes thick and serve.

Sweet pumpkkin giahni with mallow

INGREDIENTS

- 700 gr potatoes, quartered
- 700 gr sweet pumpkin cut into small pieces
- 1 bunch finely chopped dill
- 1 big onion, finely chopped
- 2 medium sized onions, thinly sliced
- 2 – 3 handfuls tender mallow cut into medium sized pieces
- 400 gr finely chopped tomato
- 1 tsp tomato paste
- 1 cup olive oil
- Salt
- Pepper

PREPARATION

1. Put into a pan the olive oil, onions, sliced potatoes, mallow and sauté them.
2. Add the tomato and the tomato paste and mix all ingredients until they blend together.
3. Half cover the food with water, add the dill, season with salt and pepper and leave it just to the boil.
4. Add the sweet pumpkin, lower the heat and leave all ingredients to boil until they are done.

Sweet pumpkin with rice (recipe no 1)

INGREDIENTS

- 400 gr rice for pilaf
- 600 gr sweet pumpkin, diced
- 1 bunch finely chopped parsley
- 4 small and tender leeks, finely chopped
- 1 big onion, finely chopped
- 1 tbsp fennel seeds
- ½ cup olive oil and as much as needed for the frying
- 1 cup of white wine (not retsina)
- Salt
- Pepper
- Some flour for the frying

PREPARATION

1. Wash, clean and cut the sweet pumpkin into small dices.

2. Season slightly the dices with salt, cover them with a thin flour coating, fry them and keep them aside.

3. Put in a pan the olive oil, onion, leeks, fennel seeds, salt, pepper, dill, mix all ingredients until they blend together and sauté them until softened.

4. Pour over the wine, leave it until all alcohol evaporates, add the sweet pumpkin and leave the ingredients to cook over low heat until all cooking liquids evaporate.

5. Put the rice into salted boiling water, leave it to boil until it is done and then drain the water.

6. Add the rice to the pan that contains the sweet pumpkin, mix all ingredients until they blend together and serve.

Sweet pumpkin with rice and peppers (recipe no 2)

PREPARATION

1. Peel the skin of the sweet pumpkin, cut it into small pieces and put it into a pan that already contains the olive oil, onions, peppers, carrots and the fennel in order to be sautéed.

2. Pour over the wine, season with pepper and salt and bring the food to the boil.

3. As soon as it comes to the boil reduce the heat and add the rice.

4. Stir gently in order to blend the rice with the other ingredients and leave everything to boil until the rice becomes soft and all water is absorbed.

INGREDIENTS

- 1 kilo sweet pumpkin cut into small pieces
- 1 bunch finely chopped fennel
- 4 green and red peppers cut into small pieces
- 2 finely chopped carrots
- 1 big onion, grated
- 1 thinly sliced onion
- 1 cup white wine (not retsina)
- 2 ½ cups rice for pilaf
- 2 cups water
- 1 cup olive oil
- Juice of 1 lemon
- Salt
- Pepper

Zucchini giahni with potatoes

INGREDIENTS

- 1 kilo medium sized zucchini cut into big rounds
- 4 big potatoes, quartered
- 2 big carrots cut into medium sized rounds
- 2 medium sized onions, finely chopped
- 1 bunch finely chopped parsley
- 400 gr finely chopped tomato
- 2 – 3 bay leaves
- 1 cup olive oil
- Salt
- Pepper

PREPARATION

1. Put in a pan the olive oil, onions, zucchini and sauté them until they get golden.

2. Add the potatoes, carrots, parsley, tomato, salt, pepper and the bay and stir until all ingredients become sautéed and blended together.

3. Half cover the food with water, reduce the heat and wait for the food to be done and for the sauce to get a smooth texture.

Stuffed zucchini flowers

INGREDIENTS

- 30 zucchini flowers
- 20 tbsp Carolina rice
- 2 medium sized onions, grated
- 1 bunch finely chopped dill
- 2 tbsp finely chopped spearmint
- 2 medium sized carrots, grated
- 1 cup olive oil
- Juice of 2 lemons
- Salt
- Pepper

PREPARATION

1. Wash the zucchini flowers and leave them to drain.

2. Put all ingredients into a big bowl, except the olive oil and lemon, and mix them until they blend together.

3. Fill the zucchini flowers with the stuffing (be careful not to be completely full in order not to open when the rice gains volume) and close them by folding the ends.

4. Place the zucchini flowers standing upright in a pan, cover them with a plate, add the olive oil, little bit of salt, pepper, the lemon juice and half cover them with water.

5. Leave them to be cooked over low heat for 20 – 30 minutes and remove the pan from the heat.

Fried zucchini flowers

INGREDIENTS

- 20 – 30 zucchini flowers
- Enough olive oil for the pan
- ½ kilo flower for the batter
- 1 tbsp oregano
- 1 teaspoon salt
- 1 egg

PREPARATION

1. Wash the zucchini flowers and drain them.
2. Put in a bowl the flower and pour little by little water until have a rather thick batter.
3. Stir the egg and pour it into the batter.
4. Add the salt and the oregano and blend the ingredients.
5. Set in fire the pan with the olive oil until it is hot.
6. Dip the zucchini flowers one by one in the batter, pour them in the hot olive oil, let them golden both sides and serve.

Fried broad beans

INGREDIENTS

- 1 kilo fresh and tender broad beans
- ½ kilo flour for the coating
- 2 eggs optionally
- 1 tbsp oregano
- Salt
- Olive oil for frying
- Water as much as needed in order to make a thick pulp

PREPARATION

1. Remove the strings of the beans, wash and leave them to drain.

2. Put the flour, salt and the oregano in a small basin and mix them until they blend together

3. Whisk the eggs and add them to the mixture.

4. Pour the water slowly – slowly while mixing the ingredients until they form a thick pulp.

5. Place the frying pan with the olive oil over the heat in order to get hot.

6. Dip the broad beans one by one to the pulp and fry them until they turn golden at both sides.

7. They can be eaten without any accompaniment but can also be served with skordalia[1].

[1] Skordalia: cream of mashed potatos and garlic or brand with olive oil, vinegar and salt.

Boiled broad beans

INGREDIENTS

- ½ kilo dried broad beans
- 1 cup olive oil
- Juice of 1 lemon
- ½ bunch parsley
- 1 finely chopped onion
- Salt
- 1 tbsp oregano

PREPARATION

1. Wash the broad beans, put them into water in order to soak for 8 – 10 hours and drain them.

2. Boil them until softened, add the salt and leave them to come to the boil several times, drain them and with the use of a small sharp knife remove their eye.

3. Place them into a bowl, add the oregano, parsley, onion, olive oil and the lemon juice, blend them in order to marinate and then

Cauliflower giahni

PREPARATION

1. Clean, cut and wash the cauliflower.

2. Fry lightly the cauliflower and keep it aside.

3. Put in a pan the olive oil, onion, garlic and the leeks, sauté them, add the cauliflower, celery, parsley and sauté them for a while.

4. Pour over the wine, let the alcohol to evaporate, add the tomato, honey and pepper, half cover with water, season with salt and leave the food over low heat until it is done.

INGREDIENTS

- 1 kilo cauliflower cut into small florets
- 4 thickly cut leeks
- 1 bunch thickly cut celery
- 1 bunch finely chopped parsley
- 2 big onions, finely chopped
- 2 – 3 finely chopped garlic cloves
- ½ cup olive oil and as much as needed for the frying
- 1 cup white wine (not retsina)
- 400 gr finely chopped tomato
- 1 tbsp honey
- Salt
- Pepper

Fried vegetables with garlic

INGREDIENTS

- 4 sliced eggplants
- 4 medium sized zucchini, sliced
- 8 green peppers
- 4 medium sized tomatoes, sliced
- 1 bunch finely chopped parsley
- 5 – 6 grated garlic cloves
- 1 tbsp oregano
- ½ cup vinegar
- Salt
- Pepper
- Olive oil as much as needed for the frying

PREPARATION

1. Clean, wash and cut the eggplants, season with salt and leave them for 1 -2 hours to lose any bitter taste.
2. Wash the eggplants with plenty of water to rinse all salt, leave to drain and fry them.
3. Fry the zucchini and the peppers.
4. Place the fried vegetables on a platter, season them with salt, whisk together the garlic and vinegar, pour the dressing over the vegetables and cover them with the tomato slices.
5. Season lightly the tomatoes with salt, sprinkle the oregano, parsley, a little bit of pepper and then serve.

Cabbage dolma[1]

PREPARATION

1. Wash the cabbage externally and with a sharp knife remove the stalk creating a cavity in the centre.
2. Put the cabbage in a pan with boiling water with the opening of the cavity facing downwards and leave it to blanch for 10 minutes.
3. Remove it from water, remove the large leaves one by one and place them into cold water.
4. Wash the rice, drain and put it into a large bowl.
5. Add the half of the olive oil for the stuffing, the rest of the ingredients and mix everything until they blend together.
6. Take one by one the cabbage leaves, cut the stalk and place over them a tablespoon of the stuffing.
7. Wrap the leaves on top of the stuffing creating thus a small parcel in the size of a thumb that is a dolma.
8. Place the dolma into a pan, one next to the other.
9. Cover them with a heavy plate, half cover them with water, add the rest of the olive oil and cook them over low heat until they are done and all water is evaporated.
10. Serve them with lemon.

INGREDIENTS

- 1 biggish white cabbage
- 500 gr rice for pilaf
- 1 bunch finely chopped fennel
- 3 tbsp finely chopped spearmint
- ½ bunch finely chopped parsley
- 2 big onions, grated
- 2 grated carrots
- Juice of 2 lemons
- 1 tbsp fennel seeds
- 1 cup olive oil
- Salt
- Pepper

[1] Stuffed cabbage or vine leaves.

Rice with cabbage

INGREDIENTS

- 1 kilo white cabbage, finely chopped
- ½ cup Carolina rice
- 2 big onions, finely chopped
- 1 bunch finely chopped parsley
- 400 gr finely chopped tomato
- 1 cup olive oil
- 1 cup red wine
- 1 tbsp honey
- 1 teaspoon nutmeg
- Salt
- Pepper

PREPARATION

1. Wash, chop and place the cabbage into a pan.

2. Add the olive oil, onion, parsley and sauté them until glazed.

3. Pour over the wine, add the tomato, rice, honey, nutmeg, season with salt and pepper, mix all ingredients until they blend together, half cover the food with water and leave it to boil over low heat until all cooking liquids are absorbed.

Magirio[1]

PREPARATION

1. Clean, wash and cut the vegetables, corn, vlita and place them into a pan.

2. Add the olive oil, onion, parsley, salt and pepper, mix all ingredients until they blend together, half cover the food with water and leave it until it is done, most of cooking liquids are absorbed and the sauce takes a smooth texture.

INGREDIENTS

- 500 gr string beans cut into medium sized pieces
- 2 zucchini cut into medium sized rounds
- 4 – 5 zucchini flowers
- 4 potatoes, quartered
- 1 – 2 vlita buds (optionally) cut into medium sized pieces
- 2 fresh corns cut into medium sized pieces
- 1 bunch finely chopped parsley
- 4 – 5 ripe tomatoes, finely chopped
- 2 big onions, finely chopped
- 1 cup olive oil
- Salt
- Pepper

[1] Cooking method used in Ikaria.

Mushrooms giahni

INGREDIENTS

- 1 kilo mushrooms, sliced
- 400 gr finely chopped tomatoes (can)
- ½ bunch finely chopped parsley
- 2 medium sized onions, finely chopped
- 4 medium sized potatoes, quartered
- 2 medium sized onions, sliced
- 4 grated garlic cloves
- 1 cup olive oil
- Salt
- Pepper
- 2 – 3 bay leaves

PREPARATION

1. Wash, clean and chop the mushrooms, onions, parsley, garlic and the potatoes and place them into the pan with the olive oil. Sauté all ingredients until softened.

2. Add the tomato, salt, pepper, bay leaves and 1 -2 cups of water, cover the pan and cook over low heat until the sauce takes a smooth texture.

Mushrooms with greens

PREPARATION

1. Remove the tough parts of the mushrooms, wash, cut into medium sized pieces and place them into a pan.

2. Add the greens, olive oil, onions, carrots, parsley, oregano, pepper, salt and sauté them until softened and slightly golden.

3. Pour over the wine and when all alcohol is evaporated add the tomato, the bay leaves and half cover the food with water.

4. Leave all ingredients to boil until the sauce takes a smooth texture.

INGREDIENTS

- 500 gr mushrooms
- 500 gr sweet wild greens, finely chopped
- 400 gr finely chopped tomatoes
- 2 sliced onions
- 2 carrots cut into rounds
- 1 bunch finely chopped parsley
- 1 tbsp oregano
- 2 – 3 bay leaves
- 1 cup olive oil
- Salt
- Pepper
- 1 cup red wine

Mushrooms with oregano and wine

INGREDIENTS

- 1 kilo sliced mushrooms
- 4 medium sized onions, sliced
- ½ bunch finely chopped dill
- ½ bunch finely chopped parsley
- 1 cup olive oil
- 1 cup white wine (not retsina)
- 4 – 5 seeds all spice
- 1 tbsp oregano
- Salt
- Pepper

PREPARATION

1. Clean, wash and chop the mushrooms

2. Place the mushrooms into a frying pan with olive oil, add the onions and sauté them until softened.

3. Pour over the wine, add the rest of the ingredients, stir, cover the frying pan and leave the food over low heat until the sauce takes a smooth texture.

Eggplants with rice

INGREDIENTS

- 300 gr rice for pilaf
- 1 kilo eggplants cut into medium sized pieces
- 1 bunch finely chopped parsley
- 3 finely chopped red peppers
- 3 – 4 grated garlic cloves
- 1 cup olive oil
- 2 finely chopped onions
- 1 tbsp oregano
- Salt
- Pepper
- Olive oil as much as needed for frying

PREPARATION

1. Wash, clean and cut the eggplants, sprinkle with salt and leave them 2 hours with the salt in order to lose any bitterness in taste.

2. Rinse the salt, drain, fry in olive oil and keep them in a colander until all olive oil is drained.

3. Put the olive oil into a deep frying pan, add the onion, garlic, peppers, parsley, oregano, pepper, little bit of salt and sauté all ingredients over low heat until softened.

4. Add the eggplants, mix everything in order to blend together, leave them 1 – 2 minutes to sauté the eggplants and remove them from the heat.

5. While sauté the vegetables, put the rice in another pan with salted boiling water, leave until it is done, drain, place on a platter and cover it with the eggplant sauce.

Eggplants with cheese

INGREDIENTS

- 1 kilo eggplants cut into rounds
- 500 gr finely chopped tomatoes
- 4 – 5 finely chopped green peppers
- 2 medium sized onions, sliced
- 4 – 5 finely chopped garlic cloves
- ½ finely chopped parsley
- 2 – 3 tbsp finely chopped spearmint
- 1 cup red wine
- ½ cup olive oil for the sauce and as much as needed for frying
- Salt
- Pepper
- 1 tbsp oregano
- 300 gr myzithra cheese

PREPARATION

1. Wash, clean and cut the eggplants, sprinkle with salt and leave them for 1 hour in order to lose any bitterness in taste.

2. Rinse with plenty of water, leave to drain for a little while, fry and place them into a colander to drain any left olive oil.

3. Put into a frying pan 1/2 cup of olive oil, add the onions, peppers, garlic, parsley, spearmint, salt, pepper and sauté them until softened.

4. Pour over the wine, add the tomatoes mix them with the rest of the ingredients and leave them until they are done.

5. Place the eggplant slices on a baking dish, sprinkle with cheese and cover them with the half of the sauce.

6. Place on top of the sauce another layer of eggplant slices, then pour over the rest of the sauce cheese and oregano and serve.

Eggplants, peppers and potatoes (tourlou)

INGREDIENTS

- 1 kilo eggplants cut into medium sized pieces
- 4 potatoes, quartered
- 4 green peppers cut into medium sized strips
- 4 red peppers cut into medium sized strips
- 2 big onions, finely chopped
- 5 -6 finely chopped garlic cloves
- 1 bunch finely chopped parsley
- 400 gr finely chopped tomatoes
- ½ cup olive oil for the sauce and as much as needed for the frying
- 2 tbsp spearmint
- Salt
- Pepper

PREPARATION

1. Wash, cut the eggplants, sprinkle with salt and leave them for 2 hours in order to lose any bitterness in taste.

2. Rinse the eggplants with plenty of water to remove the salt, drain and fry them lightly.

3. Put the olive oil, onion, garlic and the peppers into a pan and sauté them until softened.

4. Add the tomatoes, parsley, potatoes, salt, pepper and the eggplants, mix all ingredients until they blend together, reduce the heat, half cover the food with water and leave them to boil until they are done and until the sauce takes a smooth texture.

5. Ten minutes before remove the pan from the heat, add the spearmint.

Okra with tomato sauce

INGREDIENTS

- 1 kilo okra
- 4 potatoes
- 1 bunch finely chopped parsley
- 3 medium sized onions finely chopped
- 400 gr finely chopped tomatoes
- 4 – 5 finely chopped garlic cloves
- 1 cup olive oil
- 1 cup vinegar
- 1 tbsp honey
- Salt
- Pepper

PREPARATION

1. Wash the okra, top them (take care that the seeds will not be unveiled), place them into a colander and sprinkle with vinegar.

2. Put into a pan the olive oil, onion, garlic, potatos, tomatoes and sauté them until softened and golden.

3. Add one cup of water and leave them to boil for 10 minutes.

4. Add the okra, parsley, honey, season with salt and pepper.

5. Lower the heat, half cover the food with water and leave it to boil until it is done and the sauce takes a smooth texture.

Fresh peas with fennel (finokio)

PREPARATION

1. Clean, wash and cut the vegetables.

2. Put the spring onions, onions, fennel and the peas into a pan with olive oil and over low heat sauté them until the peas become soft. (If needed, add little bit of water).

3. Add the tomatoes, season with salt and pepper, mix all ingredients until they blend together, half cover them with water and leave them to boil over low heat until they are done and the sauce takes a smooth texture.

INGREDIENTS

- 1 kilo fresh peas
- 4 finely chopped spring onions
- ½ bunch thickly chopped fennel
- 400 gr finely chopped tomato (can)
- 2 medium sized onions, sliced
- 1 cup olive oil
- Salt
- Pepper

Pea soup

INGREDIENTS

- 500 gr dried peas
- 4 finely chopped red peppers
- 1 bunch finely chopped dill
- 1 big onion, crushed
- 4 finely chopped spring onions
- 1 cup olive oil or butter
- Juice of 2 lemons (optionally)
- 2 teaspoons grated nutmeg
- 1 glass white wine (not retsina)
- Salt
- Pepper

PREPARATION

1. Put the peas into a pan, cover with water and leave them to boil over low heat until they melt.
2. Process the peas in the blender until they become a smooth cream which keep aside for a little while.
3. Put into a pan the olive oil, crushed onion, spring onions, peppers and half of the dill and sauté all ingredients until slightly golden.
4. Pour over the wine, add the cream from the peas and stir with some hot water until the food becomes a veloutı.
5. Season with salt, nutmeg and pepper, sprinkle the rest of the dill and serve. Add lemon to each individual plate according to taste.

Dolma
(with vine leaves)

PREPARATION

1. Remove the stalks from the vine leaves, wash and put them into boiling water.
2. Bring them 1 – 2 times to the boil and place them into cold water.
3. Spread them one by one to a smooth surface.
4. Place the washed and drained rice into a bowl.
5. Add the onions, fennel, parsley, spearmint and cumin, season with salt and pepper, pour over ½ cup of olive oil and mix all ingredients until they blend together.
6. Spoon a small amount of stuffing on each leaf making sure that the shiny part of the leaves is facing outwards.
7. Fold the sides of the leaves and roll the dolma in the shape of a thumb.
8. Spread some leaves at the bottom of the pan in order that the dolma will not stick to it.
9. Place the dolma one next to the other forming a circle making sure that their opening is facing downwards.
10. Half cover the dolma with water, add ½ cup of olive oil, the lemon juice, season with salt and pepper and cover them with a plate. Leave them to boil over low heat until all cooking liquids are absorbed and the rice is ready.

INGREDIENTS

- 300 gr tender vine leaves and some to use for the pan
- 2 big onions, grated
- ½ cup finely chopped fennel or dill
- ½ cup finely chopped parsley
- ½ cup finely chopped spearmint
- 300 gr Carolina rice
- ½ cup olive oil for the stuffing
- ½ cup olive oil for cooking in the pan
- Pepper – cumin, grated
- Juice of 2 lemons
- Salt

Rice with tomato

INGREDIENTS

- 1 ½ cup rice for pilaf
- ½ cup olive oil
- 1 finely chopped onion
- 2 – grated garlic cloves
- 1 ½ cup grated tomato
- Coarsely crushed black pepper
- Salt
- 3 cups water
- ½ cup grated cheese
- 1 tbsp honey

PREPARATION

1. Put the olive oil, onion and garlic into a pan and sauté them.
2. Add the tomato, honey and 3 cups of water, season with salt and pepper.
3. Leave them to boil and then add the rice.
4. Stir all ingredients to avoid sticking to the pan and leave them to boil over low heat until all cooking liquids are absorbed.
5. Remove the pan from the heat and cover it with a towel until all liquids are absorbed.
6. Serve while it is hot with grated cheese on the top.

Tomato soup

INGREDIENTS

- 1 ½ kilo ripe tomatoes, grated
- 2 potatoes, boiled and mashed
- ½ bunch finely chopped celery
- ½ bunch finely chopped spearmint
- 4 – crushed garlic cloves
- ½ cup olive oil
- 1 tbsp honey
- Salt
- Pepper

PREPARATION

1. Wash the tomatoes, peel their skin, grate and put them aside.

2. Clean the potatoes, wash, boil until they are done, mash into purıe and keep them aside.

3. Put the grated tomatoes into a pan and add the celery, garlic, olive oil and honey, season with salt and pepper and leave all ingredients to boil over low heat until softened.

4. If it is necessary, add little bit of water.

5. Add the potato purıe and the spearmint and mix all ingredients until they blend together and they form a veloutı. (Add some water if that is necessary).

6. Bring them to boil and remove the food from the heat.

Dried broad beans with bulbs

INGREDIENTS

- 300 gr bulbs
- 500 gr dried broad beans
- 4 finely chopped fresh garlic
- 4 – 5 finely chopped spring onions
- 1 bunch finely chopped spearmint
- 1 tbsp oregano
- Juice of 2 lemons
- 1 cup olive oil
- Salt
- Pepper

PREPARATION

1. Clean the bulbs, wash and boil them into salted water for 15 minutes. Drain and place them into plenty of cold water for 8 – 10 hours in order to lose any bitterness in taste.

2. Put the broad beans into plenty of water for 8 – 10 hours in order to soak.

3. Boil the broad beans until they are done, not melted, drain them, remove their black eye and keep them aside.

4. Drain the bulbs and place them together with the broad beans.

5. Put the olive oil into a pan, add the spring onions and the fresh garlic, sauté them until softened, add the broad beans and the bulbs, sprinkle with the oregano and the spearmint, season with salt and pepper and pour over the lemon juice.

6. Mix all ingredients until they blend together, add 1 cup of water and bring the food to the boil for 2 – 3 times over low heat. After that, remove the pan from the heat.

Dried broan beans with lemon and oregano

INGREDIENTS

- 500 gr dried broad beans
- 500 gr sliced onions
- 3 – 4 grated garlic cloves
- 1 sprig sage
- 1 cup olive oil
- 1 tbsp oregano
- Juice of 2 lemons
- Salt
- Pepper

PREPARATION

1. Put the broad beans into plenty of water for 8 – 10 hours in order to soak.

2. Boil the broad beans with water until softened, drain them and cut their black eye.

3. Put the olive oil, onion, garlic, broad beans, oregano and sage into a pan and sauté them while stirring.

4. Pour over the lemon, add 1 cup of water, season with salt and pepper, leave all ingredients to boil so that most of the liquids get absorbed, remove from the heat and discard the sage.

Dried broad beans stifado[1]

INGREDIENTS

- 500 gr dried broad beans
- 500 gr small onions (kokaria – for stifado)
- 400 gr tomatoes grated
- 2 medium sized onions, finely chopped
- 3 – 4 bay leaves
- 1 sprig rosemary
- 7 -8 seeds all spice
- 5 – 6 finely chopped garlic cloves
- Pepper
- Salt
- 1 tbsp honey
- 1 cup olive oil
- ¼ cup vinegar

PREPARATION

1. Put the broad beans into water for 8 – 10 hours in order to soak.

2. Boil the broad beans until they are done, drain them, remove their eye and leave them aside.

3. Clean, wash the spring onions, onions and garlic, place them into a pan with olive oil and sauté them until golden.

4. Add the tomatoes, honey, broad beans and the rest of the ingredients.

5. Half cover the food with water, lower the heat and leave it until the sauce takes a smooth texture. Discard the rosemary.

[1] Method of cooking stew with small onions.

Dried beans giahni

INGREDIENTS

- 500 gr butter beans
- 400 gr finely chopped tomato
- 2 finely chopped onions
- 4 – 6 finely chopped garlic cloves
- 1 bunch finely chopped parsley
- 2 – 3 bay leaves
- 1 cup olive oil
- Salt
- Pepper

PREPARATION

1. Put the beans into plenty of water for 8 – 10 hours in order to soak.
2. Boil them in water until they are done, drain and keep them aside.
3. Put the olive oil, onions, garlic and bay leaves into a pan and sauté them until slightly golden.
4. Add the tomato and parsley, season with salt and pepper, sauté for 2 – 3 minutes, add the beans and stir.
5. Half cover the food with water and leave all ingredients to boil over low heat until they take a smooth texture.

Potatoes giahni

INGREDIENTS

- 1 kilo potatoes, quartered
- 8 small onions for stifado (kokaria)
- 1 big onion, finely chopped
- 2 carrots cut into big rounds
- 4 – 5 finely chopped garlic cloves
- 2 – 3 bay leaves
- 8 – 10 seeds all spice
- 400 gr finely chopped tomato
- 1 cup olive oil
- Pepper
- Salt
- 1 tbsp honey

PREPARATION

1. Clean, wash the onions, small onions, the garlic and place them into a pan with olive oil.

2. Sauté the ingredients, add the potatoes, washed and cut, the carrots, bay leaves and the all spice.

3. Mix all ingredients until they blend together and sauté them for a little while.

4. Add the tomato and honey, season with salt and pepper, half cover the food with water, lower the heat and leave the food until it is done and the sauce takes a smooth texture.

Potatoes with fennel (finokio) and leeks

INGREDIENTS

- 1 kilo potatoes, quartered
- ½ kilo fennel cut into medium sized pieces
- 2 leeks cut into rounds
- 2 carrots cut into thin rounds
- 1 big onion finely chopped
- 2 – 3 finely chopped garlic cloves
- 1 cup olive oil
- Juice of 1 big lemon
- Salt
- Pepper

PREPARATION

1. Wash and clean the potatoes, fennel, leeks, carrots and cut them. Finely chop the onion and garlic.

2. Place the vegetables into a pan with olive oil and sauté them.

3. When they are soft half cover them with water, season with salt, reduce the heat and leave them until they are done and they have a smooth texture.

4. At the end add the lemon juice and the pepper.

Pilaf with red sauce

PREPARATION

1. Put the rice into salted boiling water, stir and leave it over low heat until it is done.

2. Put the olive oil, onions, garlic, peppers, bay and all spice into a deep frying pan and sauté them until they get slightly golden.

3. Add the tomato paste mixed with little bit of water, the tomatoes, season with salt and pepper, leave the sauce until it becomes thick and 5 minutes before remove from the heat add the honey and stir.

4. Drain the rice, place it on a platter, pour over the sauce, sprinkle with cheese and serve.

INGREDIENTS

- 400 gr rice for pilaf
- 4 ripe tomatoes, grated
- 5 – 6 grated garlic cloves
- 2 medium sized onions, grated
- 1 tbsp tomato paste
- 2 – 3 finely chopped green peppers
- 2 bay leaves
- 1 tbsp honey
- Coarsely crushed black pepper
- 5 – 6 seeds all spice
- 1 cup olive oil or butter
- Salt
- Grated myzithra cheese

Fried peppers

INGREDIENTS

- 1 kilo long peppers (sweet or hot)
- Olive oil for frying
- Vinegar
- 6 – 7 grated garlic cloves
- 2 – 3 tbsp finely chopped parsley
- Salt
- Pepper

PREPARATION

1. Wash the peppers and leave them to drain.

2. Pierce them with a fork at two or three sides of each one, place them into a frying pan with olive oil and while covered fry them over low heat from both sides.

3. Put them on a platter and allow them to cool. Peel their skin (optionally).

4. Place them on a platter. Whisk together vinegar and garlic and pour the dressing over the peppers.

5. Season with salt and pepper, sprinkle with parsley and serve.

Chickpeas wth cabbages

PREPARATION

1. Put the chickpeas into water for 8 – 10 hours in order to soak.

2. Boil the chickpeas into water, skim off the foam and leave them to boil until they are done.

3. Drain and keep them aside.

4. Place the cabbage, washed and cut, into a pan with the olive oil and onion and sauté them until the cabbage becomes soft.

5. Pour over the wine, add the tomato, honey, parsley, fennel seeds, season with salt and pepper, half cover with water and leave the food until the cabbages are done.

6. Reduce the heat, add the chickpeas, mix all ingredients until they blend together and allow the sauce to take a smooth texture.

INGREDIENTS

- 300 gr chickpeas without the skin
- 1 kilo white cabbage or finely chopped cabbage buds
- 2 medium sized onions, finely chopped
- 1 bunch finely chopped parsley
- 1 tbsp fennel seeds
- 400 gr finely chopped tomato
- 1 cup red wine
- 1 tbsp honey
- 1 cup olive oil
- Salt
- Pepper

Soup of chickpeas

INGREDIENTS

- 500 gr chickpeas without the skin
- 2 big onions, finely chopped
- 4 tender leeks, finely chopped
- 1 sprig fresh rosemary or 1 tbsp dried rosemary
- 3 – 4 grated garlic cloves
- 400 gr finely chopped tomato (can)
- ½ cup olive oil
- Salt
- Pepper

PREPARATION

1. Put the chickpeas into water for 8 – 10 hours in order to soak.

2. Boil the chickpeas into plenty of water and while they are boiling skim off the foam.

3. When there is not any more foam on the surface of the water, add the leeks, onions, garlic and the rosemary (if use dried rosemary fold it into a piece of voile and when the food is done remove it).

4. Add the tomato, season with pepper and salt, pour over the olive oil making sure that the food is covered by water and leave it to boil until the soup is done.

Celery root with greens and potatoes

PREPARATION

1. Clean and wash all vegetables and greens and cut them.

2. Put the olive oil, onion, garlic, greens and celery root into a pan and sauté them over low heat until the greens and the vegetables become soft and the onion gets golden.

3. Pour over the wine, wait for the alcohol to evaporate, add the potatoes, dill, oregano, season with salt and pepper, pour over the lemon juice, half cover the food with water and leave it over low heat until the sauce takes a smooth texture.

INGREDIENTS

- 500 gr celery root cut into medium sized dices
- 800 – 1000 gr various wild sweet greens cut into medium sized pieces
- 4 medium sized potatoes, quartered
- 1 big onion, finely chopped
- 4 -5 grated garlic cloves
- 1 bunch finely chopped dill
- 1 tbsp oregano
- Juice of 2 lemons
- 1 cup white wine (not retsina)
- 1 cup olive oil
- Salt
- Pepper

Chards with chickpeas

INGREDIENTS

- 300 gr chickpeas
- 1 kilo chards cut into medium sized pieces
- 2 carrots cut into rounds
- 1 big onion, finely chopped
- 2 – 3 grated garlic cloves
- 1 bunch finely chopped dill
- Juice of 2 lemons
- 1 cup olive oil
- Salt
- Pepper

PREPARATION

1. Put the chickpeas into water for 8 – 10 hours in order to soak.
2. Boil the chickpeas until they are done, drain and keep them aside.
3. Clean the chards, onion, garlic, dill and the carrots, wash, cut and place them into a pan with olive oil and sauté all ingredients until softened.
4. Season with salt and pepper, half cover the food with water and leave it to boil until is done and most of the cooking liquids are absorbed.
5. Add the chickpeas, mix all ingredients in order to blend together, leave them to boil for 10 minutes and remove from the heat.
6. There must not be many cooking liquids left in the food.
7. Add lemon to each individual plate according to taste.

Skordalia from kolokasi

PREPARATION

1. Clean the kolokasi, wash and boil it until softened.
2. Drain and place it into a mortar or a blender.
3. Beat the kolokasi and garlic until they melt and add the salt.
4. Pour the vinegar and olive oil, drop by drop, and whisk them together until get a velouti cream.
5. Add some olive oil if needed.
6. It is served with fried vegetables, fish, boiled vegetables, beetroots, broad beans.

INGREDIENTS

- 500 gr kolokasi
- 1 cup olive oil
- 1/4 cup vinegar
- 4 – 5 grated garlic cloves
- salt

Soufiko[1]

INGREDIENTS

- 4 – 5 medium sized zucchini cut into medium sized pieces
- 3 – 4 eggplants cut into medium sized pieces
- 4 big potatoes cut in four
- 4 green peppers, halved
- 1 big bunch finely chopped parsley
- 4 – 5 ripe tomatoes cut into medium sized pieces
- 4 medium sized red peppers, halved
- 300 gr sweet pumpkin cut into medium sized pieces
- 1 kilo sliced onions
- 3 – 4 tb sp finely chopped spearmint
- 1 ½ cup olive oil
- Salt
- Pepper

PREPARATION

1. Wash, clean and cut the vegetables, put into a big pan layers of onions, peppers, tomatoes, potatoes, eggplants, zucchini, sweet pumpkin, parsley and spearmint, season with salt and pepper, pour the olive oil.

2. Cover the pan, lower the heat and leave the vegetables to boil gently into their own liquids until they are done and they take a smooth texture.

3. When they are done mix all ingredients and serve.

[1] Cooking method used in Ikaria.

Spinach rice

INGREDIENTS

- 1 kilo spinach cut into medium sized pieces
- 1 cup Carolina rice
- 2 finely chopped onions
- 1 bunch dill or fennel
- Juice of 2 lemons
- 1 cup olive oil
- Salt
- Pepper

PREPARATION

1. Clean the spinach, dill and onions, wash, cut and place them into a pan with olive oil to sauté them until softened.

2. Add 2 cups of water, bring to the boil, add the rice, season with salt and pepper, mix the ingredients until they blend together, lower the heat and leave the food to boil until all water is absorbed.

3. Pour over the lemon juice, stir it to be mixed with the rest of the ingredients and remove the pan from the heat.

4. Cover with a towel to allow all liquids to be absorbed and serve.

Fried kolokasi and sweet pumpkin

INGREDIENTS

- 500 gr kolokasi cut into pieces the size of a thumb
- 500 gr sweet pumpkin cut into pieces the size of a thumb
- Flour for frying
- Olive oil for frying
- Salt
- 2 tbsp oregano

PREPARATION

1. Clean the kolokasi and sweet pumpkin, wash and cut them into pieces at the size of a thumb.

2. Leave to drain and roll them into flour

3. Put the olive oil into a frying pan to become hot and fry them.

4. Drain them on kitchen paper, season with salt and sprinkle with oregano.

Split peas

INGREDIENTS

- 500 gr split peas
- 1 big onion, quartered
- 1 medium onion chopped
- 2 tbsp finely chopped parsley
- Juice of 1 lemon
- 1 cup olive oil
- Salt
- Coarsely crushed black pepper

PREPARATION

1. Wash the split peas, place it into a pan and cover with water and boil over low heat, skimming off the foam.

2. Add the quartered onion, season with salt, reduce the heat and boil the food until it becomes a thick cream.

3. Process the split peas and onion through a vegetable machine, add the olive oil, lemon juice and pepper, season with some salt if it is needed and garnish with finely chopped onion and parsley.

Lentils soup

INGREDIENTS

- 500 gr lentils
- 2 big onions, finely chopped
- 4 – 5 finely chopped garlic cloves
- 2 medium sized carrots, finely chopped
- 3 – 4 finely chopped celery stalks
- 2 – 3 bay leaves
- 400 gr finely chopped tomato (can)
- 1 cup olive oil
- Salt
- Pepper
- Vinegar (if do not add tomato, pour over vinegar to each individual plate according to taste)

PREPARATION

1. Clean, wash the lentils and place them into a pan.

2. Add the onions, garlic, carrots, celery and bay leaves, cover all ingredients with water, lower the heat and leave the soup to boil.

3. At the end add the tomato and olive oil and season with salt and pepper.

4. Leave the food to boil for 10 – 15 minutes and then remove it from the heat.

Lentils and rice soup

PREPARATION

1. Wash the lentils and rice, clean and wash the onions, garlic, carrots, parsley and celery, chop them finely, place into a pan, cover with water and leave them to boil for 10 minutes over low heat.

2. Add the bay leaves, tomato and olive oil, season with salt and pepper and leave them over low heat until they are done.

3. Add some water if that is needed.

INGREDIENTS

- 350 gr lentils
- 150 gr Carolina rice
- 2 medium sized onions, finely chopped
- 4 – 5 finely chopped garlic cloves
- ½ bunch finely chopped parsley
- 2 medium sized carrots, finely chopped
- 2 -3 bay leaves
- 400 gr finely chopped tomato (can)
- ½ cup olive oil
- 3 – 4 finely chopped celery stalks
- Salt
- Pepper

Black eyed beans with fennel (finokio)

INGREDIENTS

- 500 gr black eyed beans
- 500 gr finely chopped fennel
- 2 big onions, finely chopped
- 4 – 5 finely chopped garlic cloves
- Juice of 2 lemons
- 1 cup olive oil
- Salt
- Pepper

PREPARATION

1. Boil the beans for 10 minutes, drain them and get rid of the first water that used.

2. Put the olive oil, onions, garlic and fennel into a pan, sauté them until all ingredients become soft and the onions golden.

3. Add the beans, season with salt and pepper; half cover with water and leave them over low heat until they are done.

4. Add some water to the food, bring to the boil and serve as a thick soup into which can add lemon juice according to taste.

Dried beans with greens

PREPARATION

1. Put the beans into plenty of water for 8 – 10 hours in order to soak.

2. Boil the beans with water and keep them aside.

3. Clean, wash and cut the greens, put them into a pan, add the fennel, parsley, onions, garlic olive oil and sauté them over low heat while stirring.

4. Drain the beans, add them to the pan and keep the stock aside.

5. Add the throubi, season with salt and pepper, pour over the juice of the lemons, bring to the boil a couple of times, pour over the stock from the beans; if it is needed add some warm water in order to half cover the food and leave all ingredients to boil over low heat until they are done and only the olive oil is left to the pan.

INGREDIENTS

- 300 gr dried beans
- 1 kilo various greens (zohi, mironia, kafkalithres, galatsides) cut into medium sized pieces
- ½ bunch finely chopped fennel or dill
- ½ bunch finely chopped parsley
- 1 cup olive oil
- 2 big onions, finely chopped
- 3 – 4 crushed garlic cloves
- Juice of 2 lemons
- 1 tbsp throubi
- Salt
- Pepper

[1] Wild herb that tastes and smells like oregano.

Green broad beans giahni

INGREDIENTS

- 1 kilo seeds from green broad beans
- 2 medium sized onions, finely chopped
- 1 bunch finely chopped dill
- 400 gr finely chopped tomato
- 1 cup olive oil
- 4 medium sized potatoes, quartered
- Pepper
- Salt
- Nutmeg

PREPARATION

1. Put the olive oil, onion and dill into a pan and sauté over low heat until the onion becomes golden.

2. Add the broad beans, potatoes, tomato, season with salt and pepper, sprinkle with nutmeg, half cover the food with water and leave it to boil over low heat until it is done and the sauce takes a smooth texture.

Greens soup

INGREDIENTS

- 4 medium sized potatoes cut into small dices
- 4 finely chopped carrots
- 4 finely chopped zucchini
- 2 medium sized onions cut into slices
- 1 bunch finely chopped celery
- 1 ½ espresso cup round rice
- 2 big ripe tomatoes, finely chopped
- Juice of 2 lemons
- 1 cup olive oil
- Salt
- 2 tbsp finely chopped spearmint
- Pepper
- Nutmeg

PREPARATION

1. Clean, wash and cut the potatoes, carrots, zucchini and boil them into salted water until they are done.
2. Put the olive oil, onion and celery into a pan and sauté them until the onion becomes slightly golden.
3. Add the tomatoes, leave them to be slightly sautéed and pour over the lemon juice.
4. Add the boiled vegetables, rice, sprinkle pepper and nutmeg on top of them and cover with the stock from the vegetables.
5. Add salt if it is needed.
6. Bring them to the boil over low heat and serve them with crumbled barley rusk.
7. Garnish with fresh spearmint.

Pasta

Matsi[1] with milk

INGREDIENTS

- 250 gr matsi
- 1 kilo milk
- 2 cups water
- 1 tbsp grated nutmeg
- Salt

PREPERATION

1. Put the water into a pan in order to boil it, sprinkle salt and add the matsi.

2. Stir, lower the heat and leave them to boil until all water is absorbed.

3. Add the milk and the nutmeg and stir until get a thick soup.

4. Add some more milk, if it is needed.

5. It is served hot.

[1] A kind of Ikarian homemade tagliatelle.

Matsi with sauce

INGREDIENTS

- ½ kilo matsi
- 400 gr ripe tomatoes, grated
- 1 tbsp tomato paste
- 3 – 4 grated garlic cloves
- 2 – 3 bay leaves
- ½ cup olive oil
- 4 – 5 cloves
- Salt
- 1 tbsp honey
- Pepper
- Myzithra cheese, grated

PREPERATION

1. Put the matsi into a pan with salted boiling water and leave it to boil for 5 – 8 minutes.

2. Drain the water and place the matsi on a platter.

3. At the same time put the olive oil into a frying pan and add the garlic, bay and the cloves to gently sauté them.

4. Pour over the tomato and tomato paste with a cup of water season with salt and pepper, add the honey, bring them a couple of times to the boil until the sauce becomes thick. Pour the sauce over the matsi and serve with grated cheese.

Matsi with cheese

INGREDIENTS

- ½ kilo matsi
- 1 big onion, finely chopped
- ½ cup olive oil
- Myzithra cheese, grated
- Salt

PREPERATION

1. Put the matsi into a pan with salted boiling water, stir and leave to boil until it is done, that is about 5 – 8 minutes.

2. Drain and place it on a platter, sprinkle with cheese and mix.

3. Sauté the onion into a pan with olive oil until it becomes golden and pour the sauce over the matsi.

4. Mix all ingredients until they blend together and serve with grated cheese.

Trahanas[1] soup

INGREDIENTS

- 1 ½ cup trahana
- 2 tbsp butter or ½ cup olive oil
- 9 cups water
- 2 bay leaves
- Salt
- 1 cup myzithra cheese, grated
- Pepper

PREPERATION

1. Put the water, butter, bay and the salt into a pan and leave them to boil.

2. Add the trahana, stir to avoid the creation of any lumps and reduce the heat.

3. Leave the trahana to boil until it is done, serve into soup bowls, season with pepper and sprinkle with cheese.

[1] Wheat boiled in milk and then dried and crashed (a kind of pasta).

Meat | Game
Poultry

Boiled goat

INGREDIENTS

- 1 to 1 ½ kilo goat's meat, front part
- 4 big potatoes, diced
- 4 carrots cut into thick rounds
- 1 bunch thickly chopped celery
- 4 big onions, sliced
- 4 – 5 tbsp for soup rice
- Juice of 2 lemons
- ½ cup olive oil or butter
- Rock salt
- Pepper
- Whole meal rusks

PREPERATION

1. Wash the meat, carve into portions and boil it into a pan with water (the water should cover the meat) for 30 minutes and skim off the foam.

2. Add the vegetables, salt, olive oil and the rice and leave them to boil.

3. Season with pepper, pour over the lemon juice, add some water if it is needed in order to get a medium thick soup, and bring all ingredients to the boil.

4. It is served with whole meal rusks.

Lamb or goat with white pilaf

PREPERATION

1. Wash, carve and put the meat into a pan with water in order to boil.
2. While it is boiling, skim off the foam.
3. Add the salt and the bay leaves and leave the meat to boil until it is done.
4. Remove the meat and keep it aside.
5. Strain the stock and measure 5 cups of stock for 2 cups of rice.
6. Boil the stock into a pan, add the peppercorns and the rice and stir until it is done.
7. Add the lemon juice, butter, meat and the crushed pepper and mix all ingredients until they blend together.
8. It is served hot.

INGREDIENTS

- 1 ½ kilo lamb or goat carved into small portions
- ½ cup sheep's butter
- Juice of 2 lemons
- 2 cups rice for pilaf
- 3– 4 bay leaves
- Salt
- 1 tsp peppercorns
- ½ tsp coarsely crushed black pepper

Gamopilafo[1]

INGREDIENTS

- 1 ½ kilo goat and lamb carved into portions
- 2 medium sized onions, grated
- 600 gr ripe tomatoes, grated
- 1 tsp tomato paste
- 2 cups red wine
- 3 – 4 bay leaves
- 1 tbsp grated all spice
- 1 tsp all spice seeds
- 1 cup olive oil
- 2 cups rice for pilaf
- Salt
- 1 tsp coarsely crushed black pepper
- 5 cups stock

PREPERATION

1. Wash, carve the meat into portions and leave it to drain.
2. Place the olive oil and meat into a pan and sauté the meat until golden.
3. Add the onion and stir gently to slightly sauté it.
4. Pour over the wine.
5. Dissolve the tomato paste into the grated tomato and pour over the mixture to the meat while bringing it to the boil.
6. Add the bay leaves, all spice seeds and the pepper and cover all ingredients with water.
7. Season with salt and leave the food to boil until the meat is done. Remove the pan from the heat and with the use of a slotted spoon take out the meat and keep it aside.
8. Strain the stock, measure 5 cups of liquid and put it into the pan.
9. If cannot extract 5 cups of stock complete the liquid amount with water.
10. Place the pan with the stock over the heat in order to boil and add the all spice seeds.
11. Put the rice while stirring, lower the heat and leave it until the rice absorbs all liquid and becomes thick.
12. Serve the rice together with the meat in the same plate.

[1] This plate was prepared for the matrimonial meal.

Goat or lamb with potatoes

PREPERATION

1. Wash, carve the meat and place it into a pan that contains the olive oil and sauté until it becomes golden.
2. Add the onions and garlic, stir in order to sauté them and pour over the wine.
3. Half cover the food with water, season with salt and pepper, sprinkle with the oregano, reduce the heat and leave the meat to boil for 1 hour. (Add some more water if that is necessary).
4. Add the potatoes and the lemon juice and leave them to boil slowly until they are done and the sauce takes a smooth texture.

INGREDIENTS

- 1 ½ kilo leg or shoulder of goat carved into small portions
- 1 ½ kilo potatoes, quartered
- 2 medium sized onions, grated
- 5 – 6 grated garlic cloves
- 1 cup white wine (not retsina)
- Juice of 1 lemon
- 1 tbsp oregano
- ½ cup olive oil
- Salt
- Pepper

Goat with spaghetti

INGREDIENTS

- 1 ½ kilo goat carved into small portions
- ½ kilo spaghetti cut into thirds
- 1 big onion, grated
- 1 tbsp tomato paste
- 4 – 5 ripe tomatoes, finely chopped
- 2 – 3 bay leaves
- ½ cup olive oil
- Salt
- Pepper
- Myzithra cheese, grated.

PREPERATION

1. Put the meat and the olive oil into a pan, add the onion and bay leaves and sauté until the meat gets golden.

2. Add the tomato paste dissolved into 1 glass of water, also add the tomatoes, season with salt and pepper, half cover the food with water, reduce the heat and leave to boil until it is done. (Add some more water if that is necessary).

3. Remove the meat from the pan and place it on a platter.

4. Add little bit of water to the stock and leave it to boil.

5. Break the spaghetti, put them into the boiling stock and boil them for 10 minutes.

6. Place them on a deep platter, sprinkle with myzithra cheese and serve the food as a thick soup in the same bowl with the meat.

Goat with pilaf

PREPERATION

1. Wash, carve and put the meat into a pan.

2. Add the olive oil, onions, bay leaves and the cloves, sauté them until golden and pour over the wine.

3. Add the tomatoes, season with salt and pepper, half cover the food with water, reduce the heat and leave to boil until it is done and the sauce takes a smooth texture.

4. Put the rice into salted boiling water, stir and leave it to boil until it is done.

5. Drain the rice, place it on a platter and put the meat on top of it.

INGREDIENTS

- 1 ½ kilo goat or lamb carved into medium sized portions
- 2 medium sized onions, finely chopped
- 600 – 800 gr ripe tomatoes, grated
- 2 cups Carolina rice
- 3 -4 bay leaves
- ½ cup olive oil
- 2 cups red wine
- 4 -5 cloves
- Salt
- Pepper

Roasted goat with potatoes

INGREDIENTS

- 1 ½ to 2 kilos goat, the back part carved into portions
- 1 ½ kilo potatoes cut, quartered
- 1 cup olive oil
- Juice of 2 lemons
- 5 – 6 finely chopped garlic cloves
- Oregano
- Salt
- Pepper

PREPERATION

1. Wash the meat and place it on a roasting pan.

2. Add the potatoes and garlic, season with salt and pepper, sprinkle the oregano and mix all ingredients in order to blend together.

3. Pour over the olive oil and the lemon juice; half cover the food with water and leave it to roast gently in the oven until it is done.

Goat with fennel (finokio)

PREPERATION

1. Wash the meat, place it into a pan with the olive oil, onions, fennel and fennel root and sauté all ingredients until golden.

2. Half cover the food with water and leave it to boil for 20 – 30 minutes.

3. Season with salt and pepper, pour over the lemon juice and leave the food to boil until it is done and until the sauce takes a smooth texture.

INGREDIENTS

- 1 ½ kilo goat carved into portions
- 1 kilo fennel root and fennel cut into small pieces
- 2 sliced onions
- 1 cup olive oil
- Juice of 2 lemons
- Salt
- Pepper

Rooster with red sauce

INGREDIENTS

- 1 rooster almost 1 ½ kilo carved into portions
- 1 big onion, finely chopped
- 500 gr ripe tomatoes, grated
- 1 sprig sage (optionally)
- 1 heaped tbsp honey
- 1 glass white wine (not retsina)
- ½ cup olive oil
- Salt
- Pepper

PREPERATION

1. Wash, carve and place the rooster into a pan, add the olive oil and onion and sauté them until golden.

2. Pour over the wine, add the tomato, mix all ingredients until they blend together and reduce the heat.

3. Add the sage, season with salt and pepper, pour over the honey and half cover the food with water.

4. Leave the food to boil over low heat for 1 ½ hour until it is done and the sauce becomes thick.

5. Add some water if that is necessary.

6. It is served with pilaf, pasta, fried potatoes or mashed potatoes.

Boiled chicken with pilaf

INGREDIENTS

- 1 chicken carved into portions
- ½ kilo Carolina rice
- 1 – 2 medium sized onions, halved
- ½ cup olive oil
- 3 -4 bay leaves
- 1 heaped tbsp peppercorns
- Juice of 1 ½ lemon
- 1 tsp all spice seeds
- Salt
- Coarsely crushed black pepper

PREPERATION

1. Carve the chicken into small portions, wash and place into a pan, half cover with water, leave it to boil and skim off the foam.
2. Season the chicken with salt; add the onions and bay leaves and leave to boil until it is done.
3. Remove the pan from the heat and leave the chicken inside its stock for 20 – 30 minutes.
4. Remove the chicken, place it on a platter and cover it in order to retain its moisture.
5. Strain the stock and measure 2 ½ cups of stock for 1 cup of rice (if the stock is not enough add some water).
6. Put the stock into a pan, add the olive oil, pepper, peppercorns and the all spice, sprinkle some salt if it is needed and leave it to boil.
7. As soon as it starts boiling add the rice which is already washed and stir.
8. Leave to boil over low heat until it is done.
9. Pour over the lemon juice, stir and place on the platter with the chicken.

Chicken soup

INGREDIENTS

- 1 chicken 1 ½ kilo almost carved into portions
- 4 medium sized potatoes, quartered
- 4 medium sized carrots cut into medium sized pieces
- 2 big onions cut into thick slices
- 4 medium sized zucchini, halved
- 2 – 3 stalks celery
- 7 – 8 tbsp for soup rice
- ½ cup olive oil
- 2 lemons
- Salt
- Pepper

PREPERATION

1. Wash, carve and place the chicken into a pan.
2. Cover with water and leave it to boil.
3. Skim off the foam, add the vegetables, season with salt and leave them to boil until they are done.
4. Remove the vegetables with a slotted spoon and place them on a platter.
5. Add the necessary amount of water to the pan so that the chicken will be covered by it and leave it to boil until it is done.
6. Place the chicken on the platter with the vegetables, strain the stock and put it back into the pan in order to boil.
7. As soon as it starts boiling, add the olive oil and the rice, stir and leave all ingredients to boil until they are done.
8. If necessary, add some more water to thin the soup.
9. Serve with the vegetables and the chicken inside the plate, adding some lemon juice and pepper.

Chicken with potatoes giahni

INGREDIENTS

- 1 chicken 1 ½ kilo almost, carved into portions
- 1 kilo potatoes, quartered
- 1 medium sized onion, grated
- 2 – 3 bay leaves
- 5 – 6 all spice seeds
- 2 – 3 grated garlic cloves
- 500 gr ripe tomatoes, grated
- 1 tbsp honey
- 1 cup olive oil
- Salt
- Pepper

PREPERATION

1. Wash, cut, put the chicken into a pan, add the olive oil, onion, garlic, bay leaves, all spice and sauté until slightly golden.
2. Add the tomato and honey, mix all ingredients until they blend together and sauté for a little while.
3. Add the potatoes, season with salt and pepper; half cover the food with water, stir and reduce the heat.
4. Wait until all ingredients are done and the food takes a smooth texture.

Rabbit white stifado

INGREDIENTS

- 1 rabbit carved into small pieces
- 1 kilo medium sized onions, halved or kokaria (small onions)
- 1 cup olive oil
- ½ cup vinegar
- 1 cup white wine (not retsina)
- 1 sprig rosemary
- 1 – 2 cinnamon sticks
- 5 – 6 all spice seeds
- 2 – 3 bay leaves
- 1 tsp cloves
- Salt
- Pepper

PREPERATION

1. Wash, carve and moisten the rabbit with vinegar and leave it for 15 minutes.
2. Place the olive oil, rabbit, onions, spices and herbs into a pan and sauté until the rabbit gets golden.
3. Pour over the wine, add the salt and garlic and half cover with water.
4. Leave the food to boil until it is done and the sauce takes a smooth texture.

Rabbit red stifado

INGREDIENTS

- 1 rabbit carved into small portions
- 1 kilo sliced onions or kokaria
- 4 finely chopped garlic cloves
- 1 kilo ripe tomatoes, finely chopped
- 1 tbsp tomato paste
- 1 sprig rosemary
- 3 -4 bay leaves
- 2 – 3 cinnamon sticks
- 1 tsp cloves
- 1 tsp all spice seeds
- 1 cup olive oil
- ½ cup vinegar
- 1 cup red wine
- Salt
- Pepper
- 2 tbsp honey

PREPERATION

1. Wash, carve into portions, moisten the rabbit with vinegar and leave it for 15 minutes.
2. Place the olive oil, rabbit and onions into a pan and sauté until golden.
3. Pour over the wine, add the garlic, tomatoes, tomato paste and honey and leave all ingredients to boil for 5 minutes.
4. Add the rest of the ingredients, half cover the food with water and reduce the heat.
5. Leave the food to boil until it is done and the sauce becomes thick.
6. When it is done discard the rosemary sprig and the bay leaves.

Veal with onions

INGREDIENTS

- 1 kilo veal carved into small portions
- 1 kilo sliced onions
- 1 cup olive oil
- ½ tsp peppercorns
- ½ tsp cloves
- 1 cinnamon sticks
- 2 – 3 bay leaves
- 3 – 4 garlic cloves
- Juice of 2 lemons
- Salt
- Pepper

PREPERATION

1. Wash, cut and place the meat into a pan with olive oil and sauté until slightly golden.
2. Add the onions, spices, garlic, the bay leaves and stir while sauté them.
3. Pour over the lemon juice, season with salt and half cover the food with water.
4. Leave it to boil until the meat is done and the sauce takes a smooth texture.

Veal with potatoes

PREPERATION

1. Wash, carve and place the meat into a pan with the olive oil and sauté until slightly golden.

2. Add the onion, garlic, bay leaves and potatoes, mix all ingredients until they blend together while sauté them for 2–3 minutes.

3. Pour over the wine, add the tomatoes and honey, season with salt and pepper, half cover the food with water and leave it to boil over low heat until it is done and the sauce takes a smooth texture.

INGREDIENTS

- 1 ½ kilo veal carved into small portions
- 1 kilo potatoes, quartered
- 4 big ripe tomatoes, finely chopped
- 1 big onion, finely chopped
- 2 – 3 finely chopped garlic cloves
- 3 – 4 bay leaves
- 1 cup olive oil
- 1 cup red wine
- Salt
- Pepper
- 1 tbsp honey (optionally)

Veal with chilopites[1]

INGREDIENTS

- 1 ½ kilo veal for stew, carved into medium sized pieces
- ½ kilo chilopites
- 4 big ripe tomatoes, grated
- 1 tbsp tomato paste
- 1 tbsp honey
- 1 big onion, finely chopped
- 2 – 3 bay leaves
- 4 – 5 all spice seeds
- 1 cup olive oil
- Salt
- Coarsely crushed black pepper
- Myzithra cheese grated

PREPERATION

1. Put the olive oil and meat into a pan and sauté until golden.
2. Add the onion and mix it with the meat until softened.
3. Pour over the tomatoes and tomato paste, add the bay leaves, honey, all spice, season with salt and pepper and mix all ingredients until they blend together.
4. Half cover the food with water and leave it to boil until it is done.
5. When it is done, add some water to the pan to cover the meat and as soon as it comes to the boil add the chilopites.
6. Stir so that they will not stick to the bottom of the pan, reduce the heat and leave them to boil until they are done.
7. Serve with grated cheese.

[1] Home made pasta that looks like tagliatelle.

Veal soup

INGREDIENTS

- 1 kilo veal for stew, brisket, carved into big dices
- 300 gr rice for soup
- 2 potatoes, quartered
- 2 big tomatoes quartered
- 2 big onions quartered
- 2 – 3 celery sprigs
- 4 small carrots, halved
- ½ cup olive oil
- Juice of 2 lemons
- Salt
- Pepper

PREPERATION

1. Wash, carve and put the meat into a pan with water that covers it, leave it to boil and skim off the foam.
2. Add the salt, potatoes, onions, carrots, celery and tomatoes and leave them to boil until they are done.
3. With a slotted spoon remove the meat, carrots and potatoes and keep them aside.
4. Strain the stock and place it into a clean pan.
5. Mash the tomatoes and onions left in the colander and put them to the stock.
6. Put the pan over the heat in order to boil and add the rice, stir so that the rice will not stick to the bottom of the pan, and add some hot water in order to get a thin soup.
7. Serve the soup meat and vegetables in the same plate, pour over the lemon juice and sprinkle with pepper.

Fried veal chops

INGREDIENTS

- 4 veal chops
- 1 cup olive oil
- 1 tbsp throubi
- Juice of 2 lemons
- Salt
- Pepper

PREPERATION

1. Wash the chops and leave them to drain, season them with salt and pepper, sprinkle with throubi and leave them covered for 30 minutes.
2. Put the olive oil into a pan in order to get warm and add the chops.
3. Leave them to fry on both sides over low heat.
4. Pour over the lemon juice and season lightly with salt and pepper.

Woodcocks

INGREDIENTS

- 4 woodcocks washed and clean
- 1 cup olive oil
- 1 cup white wine (not retsina)
- 5 – 6 finely chopped garlic cloves
- Salt
- Pepper
- 1 tbsp oregano

PREPERATION

1. Put the olive oil with the woodcocks into a big frying pan and sauté them until they get golden on both sides.
2. Pour over the wine, add the garlic, oregano, season with salt and pepper and add 2 glasses of water.
3. Cover the frying pan and leave them to slightly fry until they are done and stay with olive oil.

Fried partridge with lemon juice

INGREDIENTS

- 4 partridges carved into medium sized pieces
- ½ cup olive oil
- Juice of 2 lemons
- Salt
- Coarsely crushed black pepper
- 5 – 6 all spice seeds

PREPERATION

1. Wash, clean and cut the partridges and place them into the frying pan with the olive oil.

2. Sauté the partridges until golden, add the all spice, season with salt and pepper and pour over the lemon juice.

3. Add 1 – 2 cups of water, reduce the heat and leave them until they are done and they stay with olive oil.

Thrushes in wine with oregano

PREPERATION

1. Clean and wash the thrushes, season with salt and pepper and leave them in the fridge for 1 hour.

2. Sauté the thrushes into a frying pan with olive oil until they get golden and pour over the wine.

3. Add the oregano, reduce the heat and leave them until they are done and they stay with olive oil.

4. If it is needed add some more wine.

INGREDIENTS

- 8 – 10 thrushes
- ½ cup of white wine (not retsina)
- 1 cup olive oil
- 1 tbsp oregano
- Salt
- Pepper

Fried thrushes

INGREDIENTS

- 8 – 10 thrushes
- 2 medium sized onions, sliced
- ½ cup olive oil
- 1 tsp grated cumin
- Salt
- Pepper

PREPERATION

1. Clean and wash the thrushes, leave to drain and place them into the frying pan.
2. Add the olive oil and onions and sauté them until golden.
3. Pour over the wine and season with salt, pepper and cumin.
4. Lower the heat and leave them until they are done and they stay with olive oil.
5. If it is needed, add some more wine.

Pork sausages with fried eggs

PREPERATION

1. Cut the sausages and pour them into the hot olive oil in the pan.

2. Golden them and add the eggs, salt, pepper and the spearmint, cover and let them fried until the eggs are done.

INGREDIENTS

- 4 sausages one portion each, cut in slices
- 8 eggs
- ½ cup olive oil
- Salt
- Pepper
- ½ bunch thin cut spearmint

Fried pork chops

INGREDIENTS

- 4 pork chops
- 1 cup olive oil
- 1 cup white wine
- 1 tbsp thyme or oregano
- Juice of 2 lemons
- Salt
- Pepper

PREPERATION

1. Wash the chops, leave them to drain, season with salt and place them into a frying pan with hot olive oil.

2. Fry them on both sides until golden, pour over the wine and lemon juice.

3. Lower the heat, add the pepper and thyme and leave them until they are done.

Pork in red sauce with spaghetti

INGREDIENTS

- 1 ½ kilo pork flesh carved into medium sized dices
- ½ kilo spaghetti cut into three
- 2 medium sized onions, finely chopped
- 1 cup red wine
- 5 – 6 ripe tomatoes, finely chopped
- 1 sprig rosemary
- 3 bay leaves
- 4 – 5 all spice seeds
- ½ cup olive oil
- Salt
- Coarsely crushed black pepper
- Myzithra cheese, grated

PREPERATION

1. Wash, carve and put the meat into a pan with the olive oil and onions.
2. Sauté the meat until golden, add the rosemary and all spice.
3. Pour over the wine and bring it to the boil.
4. Add the tomato, season with salt and pepper, half cover the food with water and leave it until it is done.
5. Add two glasses of water to the sauce, leave it to boil and add the spaghetti that they are cut into three.
6. Stir to prevent the spaghetti from sticking to the pan and leave them to boil inside the sauce until they are done.
7. If it is needed, add some more water.
8. Serve as a thick soup with grated myzithra cheese.

Pork with kolokasi

INGREDIENTS

- 1 kilo pork carved into portions
- 1 kilo kolokasi cut into medium sized pieces
- 2 big onions, grated
- 4 garlic cloves grated
- 2 tender leeks cut into medium sized rounds
- 2 finely chopped carrots
- 400 gr finely chopped tomatoes
- 1 bunch parsley
- 1 glass red wine
- 2 – 3 bay leaves
- 1 tsp all spice seeds
- 1 cup olive oil
- Salt
- Pepper
- 1 tbsp honey

PREPERATION

1. Wash, carve the pork, leave it to drain and place it into a pan.
2. Add the olive oil, onion, garlic, leeks, carrots and parsley and sauté until golden.
3. Pour over the wine, leave the alcohol to evaporate and add the tomato, bay leaves and all spice.
4. Wash and clean the kolokasi, cut and add it to the pan.
5. Reduce the heat, add the pepper and honey, cover them with water and leave them until they are done and a thick sauce is created.

Pork with onions

INGREDIENTS

- 1 kilo pork carved into small portions
- 1 kilo medium sized onions, sliced
- 5 finely chopped garlic cloves
- 1 sprig rosemary
- 5 – 6 all spice seeds
- 1 cup white wine (not retsina)
- ½ cup olive oil
- Salt
- Pepper

PREPERATION

1. Wash, carve and put the meat into a pan with olive oil.
2. Add the onions, garlic, rosemary, all spice and sauté until slightly golden.
3. Pour over the wine and season with salt and pepper.
4. Lower the heat, half cover the food with water and leave it until is done and it takes a smooth texture.
5. Discard the rosemary and serve.

Pork with quinces

INGREDIENTS

- 1 kilo pork or veal for stew
- 4 big quinces cut into 8 pieces each one of them
- 1 big onion, grated
- 1 cup grated tomato
- 1 heaped tbsp tomato paste
- 1 cup white wine (not retsina)
- ½ cup olive oil
- Coarsely crushed white pepper
- Salt
- 1 tbsp honey

PREPERATION

1. Wash, carve the meat into small portions, leave to drain and put it into a pan with olive oil to be sautéed.

2. Add the onion and stir gently to be sautéed with the meat.

3. Pour over the wine, bring it to the boil, add the grated tomato, tomato paste and honey.

4. Season with salt and pepper, add a glass of wine and leave all ingredients to boil.

5. Peel the skin of the quinces, cut them into big slices, discard the tough parts and seeds, wash the slices and add them to the pan with the meat.

6. Half cover with water, leave them to boil over low heat until they are done and the sauce takes a smooth texture.

Pork with turnips

PREPERATION

1. Wash, carve the meat and place it into a pan with olive oil.
2. Add the onions and turnips and sauté until the turnips become soft and the meat slightly golden.
3. Pour over the wine, wait for the alcohol to evaporate and lower the heat.
4. Half cover with water and leave the food to boil until is done and the sauce takes a smooth texture.
5. Ten minutes before remove the food from the heat, season with salt and pepper and pour over the lemon juice.

INGREDIENTS

- 1 kilo pork pancetta (or kavourma)
- 1 ½ kilo turnips, the tender parts cut into medium sized pieces
- 1 – 2 big onions, finely chopped
- Juice of 2 lemons
- 1 cup olive oil
- Salt
- Pepper
- 1 cup white wine (not retsina)

Pork with celery

INGREDIENTS

- 1 kilo pork flesh carved into medium sized pieces
- 1 ½ kilo celery and celery root cut into medium sized pieces
- 2 finely chopped onions
- 1 bunch finely chopped dill
- Juice of 2 lemons
- 1 glass white wine (not retsina)
- 2 eggs
- 1 cup olive oil
- 1 tsp grated cumin
- Salt
- Pepper

PREPERATION

1. Wash, carve, drain the meat and put it into a pan with the olive oil, onion, dill, celery, celery root and sauté them until golden.
2. Pour over the wine, add the cumin and season with salt and pepper.
3. Half cover the food with water, lower the heat and leave it until it is done and almost two glasses of stock are produced in the pan. Remove the food from the heat.
4. Whisk together the eggs and lemon juice and add into this mixture drop by drop the stock from the pan. Pour over the dressing to the food, put back the pan over the heat, bring the food to the boil and remove it from the heat.

Pork with chilopites

INGREDIENTS

- 1/1/2 kilo pork carved into dices, boneless
- 500 gr chilopites
- 500 gr ripe tomatoes, finely chopped
- 2 medium sized onions, grated
- 3 -4 garlic cloves, grated
- 1 tsp grated nutmeg
- ½ cup olive oil
- Salt
- Pepper
- Myzithra cheese, grated

PREPERATION

1. Wash, carve and put the meat into a pan with olive oil and sauté until slightly golden.
2. Add the onions garlic, tomato and nutmeg, stir gently in order to sauté them, half cover with water and leave it to boil over low heat for 45 minutes.
3. Season with salt and pepper, add water if it is necessary and leave it to boil until it is done and the sauce takes a smooth texture.
4. Put the chilopites into salted boiling water, stir and leave them to boil for 15 minutes.
5. Drain the chilopites, place them on a platter and cover with the meat. Serve with grated cheese.

Pork pihti (aspic)

PREPERATION

1. With the use of a candle burn the hair from the head and the legs.
2. Wash and put them into a pan with salted water that covers them.
3. Add the flesh and skim off the foam created when they begin to boil until the stock remains clear.
4. Leave the meat to boil, drain the stock and place it into a clean pan.
5. When the meat is cold, remove the bones, carve into small pieces and add it to the stock.
6. Add the orange and lemon juice, spices, vinegar and bay leaves.
7. Boil all ingredients for 10 minutes and allow them to cool for 15 minutes.
8. Sprinkle the pepper at the bottom of a bowl and fill it with the stock and meat. Leave it to set and preserve it in the fridge.

INGREDIENTS

- 1 pork head
- 4 pork legs
- 500 gr pork collar flesh carved into small pieces
- 1 cup orange juice
- 5 – 6 bay leaves
- 4 -5 celery sprigs
- 1 cup lemon juice
- 1 -2 tbsp vinegar
- 1 tsp green peppercorns
- 1 tsp black peppercorns
- 1 tsp grated cumin
- Salt
- Some ground pepper to sprinkle

Pork soup with trahana

INGREDIENTS

- 1 kilo pork carved into small pieces
- 2 grated onions
- 1 tsp all spice seeds
- 1 tsp peppercorns
- 2 -3 bay leaves
- 1 ½ cup sour trahana
- 1 cup olive oil or butter
- Salt
- Pepper

PREPERATION

1. Wash, carve and put the meat into a pan with water that covers it and leave it to start boiling.

2. Skim off the foam, add the salt and bay leaves and leave it to boil until it is done.

3. Remove the meat and keep it aside.

4. Strain the stock and put it back into the pan in order to boil.

5. Add the onion, olive oil or butter, all spice, pepper and trahana, reduce the heat, stir in order to break any lumps created in trahana and leave all ingredients to boil until they are done.

6. If the soup needs it, add some more water and serve with the meat inside the soup in the same bowl.

Pork tigania[1]

INGREDIENTS

- 1 kilo pork carved into medium sized dices
- 2 cups of wine
- 1 tbsp oregano
- Salt
- Pepper
- Juice of 2 lemons
- ½ cup olive oil

PREPERATION

1. Wash, carve and place the meat into a bowl to marinate with the wine, oregano, salt and pepper for 2 hours.

2. Put olive oil into the frying pan, allow it to get warm and put the meat inside to sauté.

3. Pour over the marinade, half cover with water, reduce the heat, cover and leave it to boil.

4. When all cooking liquids are gone pour over the lemon juice, cover and leave it to boil until it stays with olive oil.

[1] Cooking method used in Greece.

Roasted pork with lemon and potatoes

PREPERATION

1. Wash, carve and place the meat on a roasting pan.
2. Add the cleaned, washed and cut potatoes.
3. Season with salt and pepper, add the oregano, bay leaves, olive oil and lemon juice.
4. Clean, wash and cut the onions, garlic, add them to the food and mix all ingredients until they blend together.
5. Half cover the food with water and bake in medium hot oven until it is done.

INGREDIENTS

- 1 ½ kilo pork carved into medium sized portions
- 2 kilos potatoes, quartered
- 2 sliced onions
- 4 finely chopped garlic cloves
- Juice of 2 lemons
- ½ cup olive oil
- 1 tbsp oregano
- Salt
- Pepper
- 3 -4 bay leaves

Kavourmas[1]

INGREDIENTS

- Pork legs, only the flesh
- Pork fat (glina)
- Salt
- Oregano
- Olive oil for saute

[1] Method of ecological preservation of meat used in Ikaria.

PREPERATION

1. Remove the flesh from the bones, wash, season with salt and leave it to drain for 1 – 2 hours.
2. Place the meat with olive oil into a pan and sauté until golden.
3. Remove the pan from the heat, put the meat into a bowl and sprinkle it with plenty of oregano and salt.
4. Place the meat into a ceramic pot.
5. Melt the pork fat (glina) into a pan over low heat and pour it over the meat in the pot.
6. Cover the pot with voile and allow the contents to cool.
7. When the contents are cold, drain any liquids created in the pot.
8. Cover the pot with voile and the cap of the pot and preserve it out of the fridge during all winter season.
9. Use the meat in the same way we use any kind of fresh meat.
10. Before cooking should rinse all salt and add any salt needed to the prepared food after taste it.

Fried pork liver

INGREDIENTS

- 1 kilo pork liver cut into small pieces
- 1 cup flour
- 1 tsp grated cumin
- 1 sprig sage
- Juice of one big lemon
- 1 cup olive oil
- Salt
- Pepper

PREPERATION

1. Wash, cut and season the liver with salt.
2. Dip the liver pieces into flour and fry them in olive oil from both sides until golden and place them on a platter.
3. Strain the olive oil from the frying pan and put it into another frying pan.
4. Put it over the heat for a little while add the sage cumin, pepper, little salt, lemon juice. Leave it to become boil 2-3 times and pour it over the liver.

Snails

Snails with red sauce

INGREDIENTS

- 1 kilo snails
- 1 kilo ripe tomatoes, finely chopped
- 1 tbsp tomato paste
- 2 finely chopped onions
- 1 sliced onion
- 4 -5 finely chopped garlic cloves
- 1 cup red wine
- 3 - 4 bay leaves
- 1 tsp cumin
- 1 tsp peppercorns
- 1 cup olive oil
- Salt
- Coarsely crushed black pepper

PREPARATION

1. Clean and wash the snails from the membrane that seals their opening.

2. Put the snails into boiling water, boil for 15 minutes, drain, rinse any foam left and keep them aside.

3. Put the olive oil, onion and garlic into a pan and sauté them.

4. Add the tomatoes, tomato paste, spices, salt and bay leaves, pour over the wine and bring them to the boil for 2 – 3 times.

5. Add the snails, half cover the food with water and leave them to boil until the sauce becomes thick.

Fried snails

INGREDIENTS

- 40 big snails
- 1 cup olive oil
- 1 cup wine
- 2 – 3 tbsp vinegar
- 3 – 4 finely chopped garlic cloves
- 1 -2 rosemary sprigs
- Salt
- Pepper

PREPARATION

1. Clean and wash the membrane that seals the opening of the snails.
2. Put them into boiling water and leave to boil for 10 minutes.
3. Drain them and rinse any foam left.
4. Put the olive oil, garlic and the snails with their opening facing downwards into a frying pan.
5. Sauté for a while, add the rosemary, season with salt and pepper and stir.
6. Pour over the wine and vinegar.
7. Leave them covered over low heat allowing all cooking liquids to evaporate until they stay with olive oil.
8. When they are done discard the rosemary.

Snails with onions

INGREDIENTS

- ½ kilo snails
- ½ kilo onions cut into thick slices
- 1 bunch fennel cut into medium sized pieces
- 4 big potatoes, quartered
- Juice of 2 lemons
- 1 cup olive oil
- Salt
- Pepper

PREPARATION

1. Wash the snails and remove the membrane that seals their opening with a small knife. Boil in water for 15 minutes and drain them.

2. Rinse any foam left.

3. Put the olive oil and onions into a pan and sauté until golden.

4. Add the snails, potatoes and fennel and mix all ingredients until they blend together and gently sauté them.

5. Pour over the lemon juice, season with salt and pepper, half cover the food with water and leave it until it is done and the sauce takes a smooth texture.

Snails with potatoes

INGREDIENTS

- 50 snails
- 1 kilo potatoes, quartered
- ½ kilo ripe tomatoes, finely chopped
- 2 sliced onions
- 1 big onion, grated
- 5 -6 grated garlic cloves
- 1 cup olive oil
- 4 tbsp vinegar
- 2 – 3 bay leaves
- Salt
- Pepper
- Cumin

PREPARATION

1. Wash the snails and remove the membrane that seals their opening with a small knife.

2. Boil them into boiling water for 15 minutes, drain, rinse any foam left and keep them aside.

3. Put the olive oil, onions, garlic and potatoes into a pan and sauté them until the onion gets soft.

4. Add the tomatoes, snails, season with salt and pepper, half cover the food with water and leave it to boil over low heat for 25 – 30 minutes.

5. Add the cumin, bay leaves and vinegar and leave all ingredients for another 15 minutes to boil over low heat.

6. Add some more water if that is necessary.

Snails with bulgur[1]

PREPARATION

1. Wash the snails, remove the membrane that seals their opening with a small knife, boil them in water for 10 minutes and drain them.

2. Rinse and put them into a pan with the olive oil, garlic and onions in order to sauté them.

3. Add the tomato, honey, rosemary, season with salt and pepper and half cover the food with water.

4. Leave all ingredients to boil for 20 minutes and put the bulgur into the pan with the sauce.

5. Half cover with water reduce the heat and leave it to boil while constantly stirring to prevent from sticking to the pan and until the food becomes slightly thick. (Add some more water if that is necessary).

INGREDIENTS

- ½ kilo snails
- 1 kilo ripe tomatoes, finely chopped
- 2 big onions, finely chopped
- 2 – 3 finely chopped garlic cloves
- ½ kilo bulgur
- 1 cup olive oil
- 1 – 2 rosemary sprigs
- 1 tbsp honey
- Salt
- Pepper

[1] Crashed wheat.

Fish | Seafood

Lobster with lemon and olive oil

INGREDIENTS

- 1 ½ - 2 kilo lobsters
- 1 cup olive oil
- Juice of 2 lemons
- Some rock salt
- Pepper
- Some string and little cotton

PREPARATION

1. Wash the lobsters and seal with cotton the opening of their belly.
2. Tie with the string their tails on their bodies and put them into salted boiling water.
3. The water should cover the lobsters.
4. Boil them for 40 – 45 minutes.
5. Remove the lobsters from the pan and leave them to cool.
6. Cut their legs and empty them from their flesh.
7. Separate the head from the body and remove the flesh.
8. Cut the flesh into small pieces, place them on a platter, pour over them the lemon juice and olive oil and sprinkle them with pepper.

Kakavia[1]

PREPARATION

1. Clean and wash all fish and vegetables.

2. Put the vegetables into a pan and on top of them place the fish, one tightly next to the other so that they will not dissolve during their boiling.

3. Add the celery, all spice, pepper, olive oil, tomato and lemon juice, half cover the food with water and leave it to boil over low heat for 30 – 35 minutes.

4. Remove cautiously the fish and vegetables from the stock and place them on a platter.

5. Strain the stock and serve it into a deep bowl together with the fish and vegetables.

INGREDIENTS

- 1 ½ kilo various fish
- 5 – 6 small or big onions, quartered
- 4 carrots cut into medium sized rounds
- 4 potatoes, quartered
- 2 ripe tomatoes, grated
- 2 celery sprigs
- Juice of 2 lemons
- 1 cup olive oil
- 1 tsp all spice
- ½ tsp peppercorns
- Salt
- Coarsely crushed black pepper

[1] Cooking method for fish soup.

Squids with fennel (finokio)

INGREDIENTS

- 1 kilo squids cut into pieces
- 1 kilo fennel cut into medium sized pieces
- 5 finely chopped spring onions
- 400 gr finely chopped tomato (can)
- 1 cup olive oil
- Salt
- Pepper

PREPARATION

1. Wash, clean, cut the squids and place them into a pan together with the olive oil, spring onions and fennel in order to sauté them until softened.

2. Add the tomato, season with salt and pepper, half cover the food with water, bring it to the boil, reduce the heat and leave all ingredients to boil until they are done and the sauce takes a smooth texture.

Squids with fennel (finokio) and potatoes

INGREDIENTS

- 1 kilo squids cut into small pieces
- 4 potatoes, quartered
- 500 gr thickly chopped fennel
- 2 big onions, finely chopped
- 4 big ripe tomatoes, grated
- 1 cup olive oil
- Salt
- Pepper

PREPARATION

1. Clean, wash, cut the squids and place them into a pan.

2. Add the onion, olive oil and sauté them over medium heat until slightly golden.

3. Add the fennel, potatoes, stir until the fennel becomes soft, then add the tomato, season with salt and pepper and mix all ingredients until they blend together.

4. Half cover the food with water and leave them to boil over medium heat until they are done and the sauce becomes thick.

Fried squids

INGREDIENTS

- 1 kilo squids cut into rounds or whole small squids
- Flour for frying
- Olive oil for frying
- Salt
- Juice of 2 lemons

PREPARATION

1. Clean the squids and if they are big cut in small pieces, wash and leave them to drain. Season with salt and leave them with the salt for 15 minutes.

2. Place the frying pan with olive oil over the heat to get warm.

3. Put the flour into a bowl and roll the squids on it one by one.

4. Toss them little bit so that they will lose any excess of flour and put them into the frying pan.

5. Fry them over medium heat until softened and golden on every side.

6. Cover a platter with kitchen paper in order to drain the squids which place on top of it.

7. Serve them on a platter and pour over them the lemon juice.

Mullet with potatoes

PREPARATION

1. Clean, cut, wash the fish, pour over them the lemon juice, season with salt and keep them aside.

2. Put into a pan the olive oil with the onions and gently sauté them.

3. Add the potatoes, bay leaves, tomatoes and parsley and mix all ingredients until they blend together.

4. Arrange the fish on top of the ingredients, sprinkle with spearmint, season with salt and pepper, half cover the food with water and lower the heat.

5. Leave them to be cooked until they are done and the sauce takes a smooth texture.

INGREDIENTS

- 1 ½ kilo mullets (discard the heads)
- 1 kilo potatoes cut into rounds
- 2 onions cut into rounds
- 4 ripe tomatoes, finely chopped
- ½ bunch finely chopped parsley
- 3 -4 bay leaves
- 1 cup olive oil
- ½ bunch finely chopped spearmint
- Juice of 1 lemon
- Salt
- Coarsely crushed black pepper

Mackerel in olive oil and oregano

INGREDIENTS

- 1 kilo mackerels
- 2 big onions, sliced
- 1 bunch finely chopped fennel or dill
- ½ bunch finely chopped parsley
- 3 – 4 finely chopped garlic cloves
- 1 cup olive oil
- Juice of 2 lemons
- 1 tbsp oregano
- Salt
- Pepper

PREPARATION

1. Clean, wash the mackerels and place them into a big frying pan.

2. Add the olive oil, onions, garlic, dill, parsley, lemon juice, oregano, and season with salt and pepper. also add two glasses of water.

3. Cover the frying pan and leave all ingredients to simmer until they stay with their olive oil.

Mackerels plaki[1]

INGREDIENTS

- 1 – 1 ½ kilo mackerels
- 1 kilo grated tomatoes
- 2 big onions, finely chopped
- 3 – 4 finely chopped garlic cloves
- 1 bunch finely chopped parsley
- 1 cup red wine
- 1 cup olive oil
- Salt
- Pepper
- 3 -4 bay leaves

PREPARATION

1. Clean and wash the mackerels.

2. Place the fish the one next to the other into a broad pan.

3. Add the onions, parsley, garlic, tomatoes, bay leaves, season with salt and pepper and pour over the wine and olive oil.

4. Half cover the food with water and leave it to simmer until it is done and the sauce takes a smooth texture.

[1] Cooking method used in many parts of Greece.

Cod with onions

INGREDIENTS

- 1 kilo salt cod cut into small portions
- 1 kilo onions, sliced
- 1 cup olive oil
- 1 cup white wine (not retsina)
- Juice of 2 lemons
- 4 – 5 peppercorns
- 1 rosemary sprig
- Salt
- Pepper

PREPARATION

1. Wash well the cod to remove the excessive salt, cut it into small portions and place it into a bowl with plenty of water for 24 hours while frequently changing the water.

2. Put the olive oil, onions, rosemary and peppercorns into a pan and sauté them until slightly softened.

3. Pour over the wine, add the fish, lemon juice, pepper, half cover the food with water and leave it to simmer for 10 minutes.

4. Taste the sauce and season with salt.

5. Leave the food to simmer over low heat until it is done and it stays with its sauce.

Cod with tomatoes and peppers

INGREDIENTS

- 1 kilo salt cod cut into portions
- 1 kilo tomatoes, sliced
- 4 green peppers cut into medium sized pieces
- 4 red peppers cut into medium sized pieces
- 1 bunch finely chopped spearmint
- 1 bunch finely chopped parsley
- 4 finely chopped garlic cloves
- 4 sliced onions
- 1 cup olive oil
- Salt
- Pepper

PREPARATION

1. Wash the cod with lukewarm water, cut and place it into a bowl with plenty of water for 24 – 30 hours while frequently changing the water.

2. Spread half of the onions to the bottom of pan and also place into it half of the peppers, half of the tomatoes, half of the garlic half of the parsley spearmint and the cod.

3. Add the rest of onions, peppers, tomatoes, garlic, spearmint, parsley.

4. Pour over the olive oil, season with pepper, half cover the food with water and leave all ingredients to boil until they are done and the sauce takes a smooth texture.

5. Taste the sauce and add salt if that is needed.

Cod with potatoes

PREPARATION

1. Cut and wash the cod with lukewarm water to rinse off the salt.

2. Place the cod into a bowl with plenty of water for 24 – 30 hours while frequently changing the water.

3. Put into a pan the olive oil, onions, garlic, parsley and potatoes and sauté while stirring until the onion becomes golden.

4. Add the tomato, bay leaves, all spice and honey and mix all ingredients until they blend together.

5. Arrange the cod on top, half cover the food with water, sprinkle with pepper and leave it to boil until it is done and the sauce takes a smooth texture.

6. Taste the sauce and add salt if that is needed.

INGREDIENTS

- 1 kilo cod cut into small pieces
- 1 kilo potatoes, quartered
- 400 gr finely chopped tomatoes, can
- 1 cup olive oil
- ½ bunch finely chopped parsley
- 2 big onions, finely chopped
- 3 – 4 bay leaves
- 5 -6 all spice seeds
- 3 – 4 finely chopped garlic cloves
- Salt
- Pepper
- 1 tbsp honey

Cod with wild greens

INGREDIENTS

- 1 salt cod almost 1 kilo cut into medium sized portions
- 1 – 1 ½ kilo wild greens (kafkalithres, mironia, zohos)
- 5 finely chopped spring onions
- Juice of 2 lemons
- 1 cup olive oil
- 1 bunch finely chopped dill
- Salt
- Pepper

PREPARATION

1. Cut the cod into portions, rinse the excess salt and place it into a bowl with plenty of water for 24 hours while frequently changing the water.

2. Clean, wash, cut the greens, dill, spring onions and put them into a pan with olive oil in order to sauté them until softened.

3. Mix all ingredients to blend together and arrange on top of them the cod.

4. Half cover the food with water and leave it to boil for 10 minutes so that the cod discards the rest of the remaining salt.

5. Taste the stock from the pan and add salt, pepper and lemon juice.

6. Leave the food to boil until it is done and it stays with little cooking liquid and olive oil.

Cod skordalia

PREPARATION

For the cod see: FRIED COD.

FOR THE SKORDALIA

1. Boil the potatoes, peel and mash them.
2. Soak the bread crumb, squeeze it to drain and keep it aside.
3. Put the garlic into a mortar and melt it with two table spoons of olive oil.
4. Add the crumbs and beat them until they melt.
5. Add the mashed potatoes, the rest of the olive oil, salt and vinegar and beat all ingredients until they form a smooth cream.
6. If more liquid is needed, add olive oil or vinegar according to taste.
7. It also accompanies other fish, beetroots, broad beans and fried vegetables.

INGREDIENTS

- 1 kilo salt cod cut into portions
- Olive oil for frying
- Flour for the coating of the cod

FOR SKORDALIA

- ½ kilo crumbs from stale bread
- 5 – 6 grated garlic cloves
- Olive oil almost 1 cup
- 2 big potatoes, boiled and peeled
- 4 – 5tbsp vinegar
- Salt

Fried cod

INGREDIENTS

- 1 kilo salt cod
- 1 ½ cup flour
- Olive oil for frying

PREPARATION

1. Cut the cod into small portions, wash it with lukewarm water and place it in a bowl with plenty of water for 24 – 30 hours to discard all of its salt, while changing frequently the water.
2. Rinse the cod and leave it to drain.
3. Put the flour into a bowl and stir some water until get a thick pulp.
4. Place the frying pan with olive oil over the heat to get warm.
5. Dip the cod in the pulp and put it into the frying pan.
6. Fry it from both sides until golden.
7. It is served hot.

Balades[1] with lemon

INGREDIENTS

- 1 kilo balades
- 4 carrots cut into slim sticks
- 4 sliced onions
- 2 tbsp finely chopped parsley
- 1 cup olive oil
- 1 cup white wine (not retsina)
- Juice of 2 lemons
- 3 – 4 bay leaves
- Salt
- Pepper

PREPARATION

1. Clean, wash the fish and keep them aside.

2. Clean, wash the onions, carrots and parsley, cut and place them into a frying pan with the olive oil and bay leaves to be gently sautéed.

3. Pour over the wine, add one glass of water and allow the carrots to become tender.

4. Add the fish and lemon juice, season with salt and pepper and leave them to simmer over low heat for 15 minutes.

5. Add some more water if that is needed.

[1] Type of fish found in the Mediterranean sea.

Red mullet with wine

INGREDIENTS

- 1 kilo red mullets
- 1 cup olive oil
- 4 medium sized onions, sliced
- 3 tender leeks, finely chopped
- 4 – 5 grated garlic cloves
- 1 bunch finely chopped dill
- Juice of 2 lemons
- 1 ½ glass of water white wine (not retsina)
- Salt
- Pepper

PREPARATION

1. Put the onions, leeks, dill, garlic and olive oil into a broad pan and sauté them until softened.

2. Clean, wash the fish, arrange them the one next to the other on top of the sautéed vegetables. Pour over the wine.

3. Season with salt and pepper, pour over the lemon juice, cover the pan and leave them to simmer over low heat for 15 – 20 minutes until they stay with olive oil.

4. Pour little bit more wine if that is necessary.

Fried red mullets

PREPARATION

1. Clean, wash the fish, leave them to drain and season with salt.

2. Place the frying pan with olive oil over the heat to get warm.

3. Spread the flour on a big plate and coat the fish with it.

4. When the olive oil is hot, place the fish into the frying pan and fry from both sides until golden.

5. Place the fish on a platter.

6. Strain the olive oil from the frying pan and put it into another frying pan.

7. Put it over the heat to be hot, add the rosemary and lemon juice, leave it for two minutes and pour it over the fish.

INGREDIENTS

- 1 kilo red mullets
- Flour for frying
- Olive oil for frying
- Juice of 2 lemons
- Salt
- 1 rosemary or sage sprig (optionally)

Fried fish savoro[1]

INGREDIENTS

- 1 ½ kilo fish for frying
- 1 ½ cup olive oil
- ½ cup vinegar
- 3 – 4 finely chopped garlic cloves
- 1 tbsp tomato paste
- 1 rosemary sprig
- 2 – 3 bay leaves
- 4 tbsp flour
- 1 ½ glass water
- 1 tsp honey
- Pepper
- Salt
- Flour for frying

PREPARATION

1. Clean, wash the fish, season them with salt and leave them into a colander to drain.
2. Put the olive oil into a frying pan to get hot, coat the fish with flour and fry them until golden.
3. Place them on a platter and strain the olive oil from the frying pan.
4. Wash the frying pan and put the strained olive oil into it. Add little bit of olive oil.
5. Allow the olive oil to get hot, add the flour, rosemary and bay leaves and stir the ingredients in order to sauté them.
6. Stir in the tomato paste dissolved in a glass of water, vinegar, garlic, season with salt and pepper, add the honey and stir until the sauce becomes thick.
7. Pour the sauce over the fish and leave them to marinate for 10 minutes. Serve.

[1] Cooking method used in the Greek islands.

Fish white savoro

PREPARATION

Use the same ingredients as in "Fried Fish Savoro". Follow the same preparation procedure excluding the use of tomato paste.

Pilaf with sea shells

INGREDIENTS

- 1 kilo sea shells
- 4 big ripe tomatoes, grated
- 1 cup rice for pilaf
- 2 finely chopped onions
- 2 – 3 grated garlic cloves
- 1 cup olive oil
- 2 tbsp finely chopped spearmint
- Salt
- 5 – 6 peppercorns and some ground black pepper
- 2 ½ cups water

PREPARATION

1. Wash the sea shells and rinse the remaining sand of them.

2. Put the olive oil, onion, garlic and sea shells into a pan and sauté them until the onion becomes slightly golden.

3. Add the tomato, spearmint, season with salt and pepper mix the ingredients and bring them to the boil for one couple of times.

4. Add 2 ½ cups of water, leave them to boil, add the rice and mix all ingredients until they blend together. Leave the food to boil over low heat until it becomes thick.

Cuttlefish with wine

INGREDIENTS

- 1 kilo cuttlefish cut into medium sized pieces
- 2 grated onions
- 1 ½ cup red wine
- 1 cup olive oil
- 2 – 3 bay leaves
- 1 tbsp throubi
- Salt
- Coarsely crushed black pepper

PREPARATION

1. Remove the hard shell and intestines from the cuttlefish, wash and cut them into medium sized pieces.

2. Place the cuttlefish into a deep frying pan with a cap, add the olive oil, onions, one cup of water, cover them and leave them to boil over low heat until they are done and they stay with olive oil.

3. Add the bay leaves, throubi, season with salt and pepper and pour over the wine.

4. Add a glass of water and leave the food to simmer over low heat until it stays with olive oil.

Cuttlefish with fennel (finokio)

INGREDIENTS

- 1 kilo cuttlefish cut into small pieces
- 1 kilo fennel cut into medium sized pieces
- 2 finely chopped onions
- Juice of 2 lemons
- 1 cup olive oil
- 1 cup white wine (not retsina)
- Salt
- Coarsely crushed black pepper

PREPARATION

1. Clean, wash, cut the cuttlefish and keep them aside.

2. Clean, wash, cut the onions and fennel and place them into a pan with olive oil to sauté them until softened.

3. Add the cuttlefish, season with salt and pepper and stir all ingredients in order to sauté them.

4. Pour over the wine, wait for the alcohol to evaporate, half cover with water, pour over the lemon juice and leave the food to simmer over low heat until it is done and it stays with olive oil.

Cuttlefish with tomato

INGREDIENTS

- 1 kilo cuttlefish cut into small pieces
- ½ kilo ripe tomatoes, grated
- 1 tbsp tomato paste
- 1 big onion, grated
- 3 – 4 grated garlic cloves
- 1 cup olive oil
- 1 cup red wine
- 1 tbsp fennel seeds
- 1 tsp all spice seeds
- Salt
- Pepper

PREPARATION

1. Remove the hard shell, intestines and the eyes from the cuttlefish.

2. Wash the cuttlefish and cut them.

3. Put the olive oil, onions, garlic and cuttlefish into a pan and sauté them until softened.

4. Pour over the wine, allow the alcohol to evaporate, add the tomato paste, tomatoes, fennel seeds, all spice, season with salt and pepper.

5. Cover the food with water and leave it to simmer over low heat until the cuttlefish is done and the sauce takes a smooth texture.

Cuttlefish with rice

INGREDIENTS

- 1 kilo cuttlefish cut into small pieces
- 1 cup rice
- 2 finely chopped onions
- 1 bunch finely chopped dill
- 1 cup olive oil
- 4 big ripe tomatoes, grated
- 1 tsp cumin
- Salt
- Pepper

PREPARATION

1. Clean, wash, cut the cuttlefish and place them into a pan with olive oil and onions to sauté them until slightly golden.

2. Add the tomato, dill, cumin, season with salt and pepper and mix all ingredients until they blend together.

3. Half cover the food with water, bring it to the boil, reduce the heat and leave it to boil until it is done and 2 ½ cups of water remain in the pan.

4. Add the rice stir and leave it to boil until it is done and all cooking liquids are gone.

5. Add some warm water if that is needed.

Cuttlefish with their ink

INGREDIENTS

- 1 kilo cuttlefish cut into small pieces
- 1 big onion, grated
- 2 cups finely chopped finokio
- 2 tbsp finely chopped dill
- Juice of 1 big lemon
- 1 cup olive oil
- 1 tbsp fennel seeds
- 1 cup white wine (not retsina)
- Salt
- Pepper

PREPARATION

1. Remove the hard shell and intestines from the cuttlefish and keep 4 small bags of ink.

2. Wash and cut the cuttlefish into small pieces.

3. Put the olive oil, onions, cuttlefish, finokio, dill and fennel seeds into a pan and sauté them until golden.

4. Pour over the wine and bring the food to the boil for 2 – 3 times.

5. Half cover the food with water and leave it to simmer over medium heat for 30 minutes.

6. Add the ink, season with salt and pepper, pour over the lemon juice, mix all ingredients until they blend together, add 1 – 2 glasses of water and leave the food to simmer until the cuttlefish is done and it stays with olive oil.

Octopus with onions (stifado)

INGREDIENTS

- 1 – 1 ½ kilo octopus
- 1 kilo onions cut into thick slices
- 1 kilo fresh ripe tomatoes, finely chopped
- ½ tbsp tomato paste
- 1 cup red wine
- 1 cup olive oil
- 3 – 4 bay leaves
- 1 rosemary sprig
- 3 – 4 finely chopped garlic cloves
- Salt
- Coarsely crushed black pepper

PREPARATION

1. Wash the octopus and put it into a pan with one cup of water.

2. Leave it to boil over low heat until it is done.

3. Cut it into medium sized pieces, rinse off the foam and place it into a pan with the olive oil, onions, garlic, bay leaves and rosemary and stir all ingredients while sauté them.

4. Pour over the wine and add the tomato, season with salt and pepper, half cover the food with water and leave it over low heat until it is done and it takes a smooth texture.

Octopus with macaroni

INGREDIENTS

- 1 kilo octopus
- ½ kilo macaroni
- 4 big ripe tomatoes, grated
- 1 cup olive oil
- 1 cup white wine (not retsina)
- 2 – 3 bay leaves
- 1 big onion, finely chopped
- Salt
- 5 – 6 peppercorns and 1 tsp ground black pepper

PREPARATION

1. Clean, wash and cut the octopus into small pieces.

2. Put it into a pan with the olive oil, onion, bay leaves and peppercorns in order to sauté the ingredients over low heat until slightly golden.

3. Pour over the wine and bring the food to the boil for 2 – 3 times until the alcohol is evaporated.

4. Add the tomato, ground pepper, salt, 1 – 2 cups of water and leave the food to boil over low heat until the octopus becomes soft.

5. Count the liquid inside the pan and add some more water which in total it should be around 7 cups.

6. Leave the food to boil, add the macaroni, mix the ingredients and leave them to boil over low heat for 10 – 12 minutes.

Octopus with rice

INGREDIENTS

- 1 ½ kilo octopus cut into small pieces
- 2 finely chopped onions
- 4 big ripe tomatoes, grated
- 1 cup for pilaf rice
- 1 cup olive oil
- 1 cup white wine (not retsina)
- 2 ½ cups stock
- 3 – 4 bay leaves
- Salt
- Coarsely crushed black pepper

PREPARATION

1. Clean, wash, cut the octopus and put it into a pan.

2. Add the olive oil, onions, bay leaves and leave them to sauté until slightly golden. Pour over wine, allow the alcohol to evaporate and add the tomato, season with salt and pepper.

3. Mix all ingredients until they blend together, half cover the food with water and leave it to boil over low heat until the octopus becomes soft.

4. Measure the stock in the pan which should be 2 ½ cups. Add some more water if that is necessary, bring the food to the boil and add the rice.

5. Stir in the rice to blend with the rest of the ingredients and leave it to boil over low heat until it becomes pilaf.

6. Discard the bay leaves and serve.

Octopus in vinegar

INGREDIENTS

- 1 – 1 ½ kilo octopus cut into small pieces
- 1 cup olive oil
- ½ cup vinegar
- 1 tbsp oregano
- Coarsely crushed black pepper

PREPARATION

1. Wash and clean the octopus.
2. Put it into a pan with one cup of water and leave it to simmer over low heat until it is done.
3. Rinse off the foam and the blackened skin.
4. Leave it to drain, cut it into medium sized pieces and put it into a bowl.
5. Whisk together the olive oil, vinegar and oregano and pour the dressing over octopus.
6. Sprinkle with pepper and serve.

Fish with oregano

INGREDIENTS

- 1 kilo fish (blackfish, sea breams, balades, saddled breams, red mullets)
- 1 cup olive oil
- Juice of 2 lemons
- 2 sliced onions
- 1 bunch finely chopped parsley
- Salt
- Pepper

PREPARATION

1. If you have a big fish cut it into slices just after clean and wash it.

2. Put the olive oil and onions into a big frying pan and sauté them.

3. Arrange the fish the one next to the other, season with salt, sprinkle with oregano, pour over the lemon juice, add the pepper and parsley, half cover with water, cover the frying pan and leave them to simmer over medium heat until they are done and they stay with olive oil.

Fried fish

INGREDIENTS

- 1 – 1 ½ kilo fish for frying (anchovies, sardines, red mullets, tiddlers)
- 1 – 1 ½ cup flour
- Olive oil for frying
- Salt
- Lemons

PREPARATION

1. Clean, wash the fish, season them with salt and leave them with this salt for 30 minutes.

2. Put the flour on a platter and mix it with some salt.

3. Place the frying pan over the heat, add the olive oil to become warm, dip the fish one by one to the flour and put them into the frying pan.

4. Fry them on both sides until golden and place them on a platter.

5. Pour lemon juice over them and serve hot.

Fish soup

INGREDIENTS

- 1 1 /2 kilo fish suitable for boiling
- 4 medium sized potatoes, quartered
- 4 medium sized zucchini cut into big rounds
- 4 carrots, halved
- 2 small onions
- 2 stalks celery
- 2 – 3 ripe tomatoes, quartered
- Juice of 2 – 3 lemons
- 1 cup round rice
- 1 cup olive oil
- Salt
- Pepper

PREPARATION

1. Clean, wash the fish and vegetables.
2. Put the vegetables into a pan and on top of them arrange the fish.
3. Add the salt, half of the olive oil, cover the food with water and leave it to boil for 20 – 30 minutes until it is done.
4. Remove the fish and vegetables, place them on a platter, and pour over them the rest of the olive oil and ½ of the lemon juice.
5. Strain the stock and measure 6 – 7 cups of it. (If necessary add more water).
6. Put the stock into a pan to boil and add the rice.
7. Stir the rice and leave it to boil for 20 – 25 minutes.
8. Add the rest of the lemon juice, some salt if it is needed, pepper and serve with the fish and vegetables.

Shellfish

Sea urchins

INGREDIENTS

- Sea urchins
- Lemon

PREPARATION

1. Make sure that the sea urchins are freshly collected and they have lived in clean waters.

2. Take them carefully one by one and with the use of a knife cut them on top.

3. Remove their intestines and keep only their eggs into a bowl.

4. Sprinkle them with lemon and eat them right away.

Shellfish with lemon

PREPARATION

1. Clean the shellfish, wash and boil them in salted water.

2. Drain and put them into a bowl, sprinkle with olive oil and lemon juice.

INGREDIENTS

- 1 ½ - 2 kilos shellfish (clams, barnacles, cockles etc.)
- 1 cup olive oil
- Juice of 2 lemons
- Salt

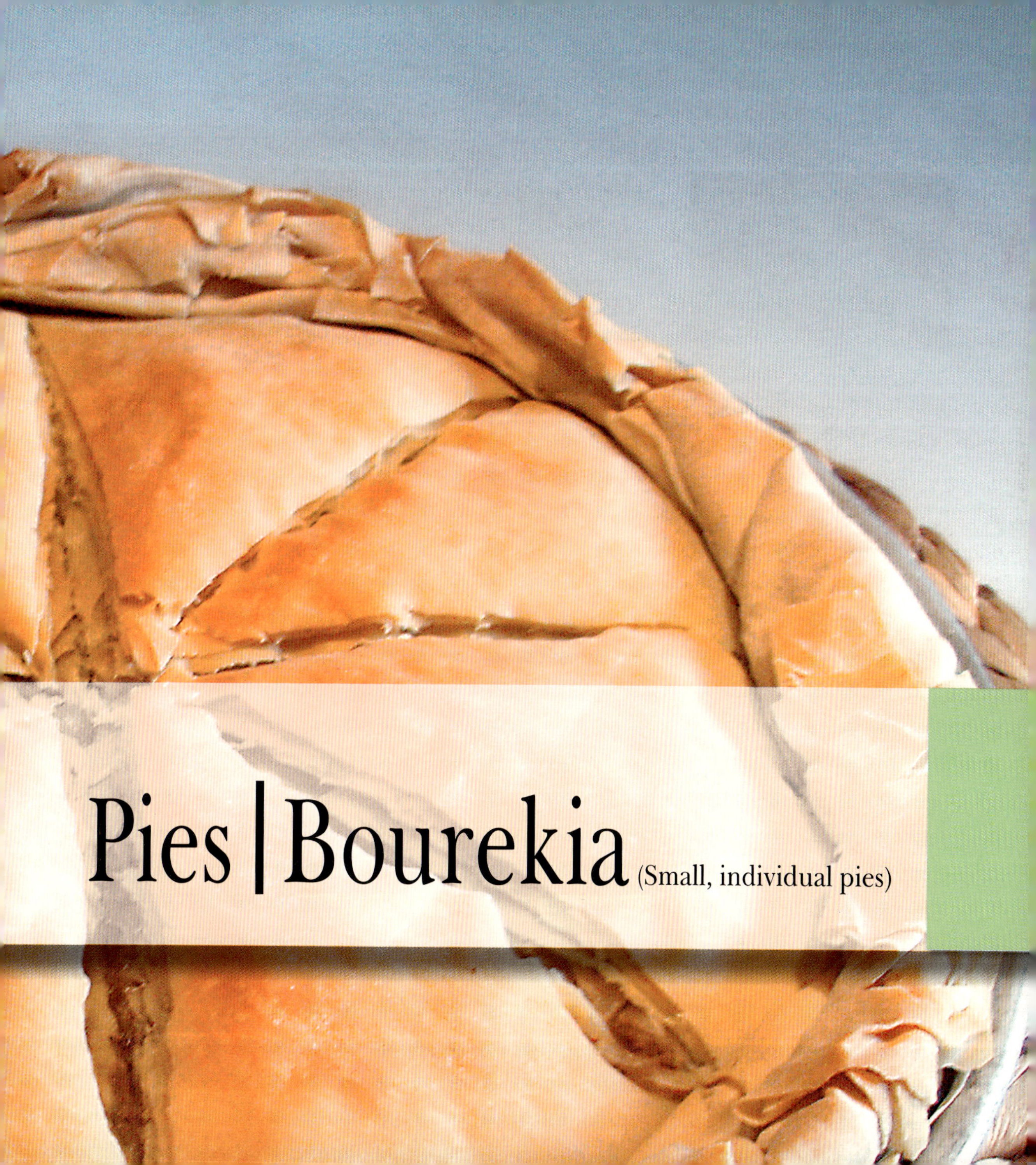

Pies | Bourekia (Small, individual pies)

Bourekia with aromatic greens

INGREDIENTS

FOR THE FILLING

- 1 kilo wild greens (mironia, kafkalithres), finely chopped
- 4 – 5 finely chopped leeks, only the white part
- 1 bunch finely chopped dill
- 1 big onion, finely chopped
- 5 – 6 finely chopped spring onions
- ½ cup olive oil
- 250 gr myzithra cheese, grated
- Salt
- Pepper

FOR THE FILO

- 1 kilo flour for all uses
- Flour for flouring
- Lukewarm water for the dough
- Olive oil for frying

PREPARATION

1. Clean, wash and cut the greens, leeks, onion, spring onions and dill.
2. Place all the ingredients into a big pan with olive oil.
3. Place the pan over the heat and sauté the ingredients until all cooking liquids evaporate and become slightly golden.
4. Remove the pan from the heat, leave the contents to cool stir in the cheese to blend with the rest of the ingredients and add some salt if it is needed.
5. Put into a small basin the flour and salt, make a well in the middle and pour over the water slowly and knead until get soft dough that does not stick on your hands.
6. Leave the dough covered with a towel for about 30 minutes in order to stand and later divide it by forming medium sized balls by it.
7. Roll the dough, dust flour on it and with the use of a glass cut it into small circles.
8. Put a tea spoon of filling in the middle of each circle and fold it.
9. Press the edges with your fingers and fry the bourekia in hot olive oil until golden.

Bourekia with fennel (finokio)

PREPARATION

1. Clean, wash and cut the fennel, onions, leeks and place them into a big pan to be sautéed until all cooking liquids evaporate and they get golden.
2. Season with pepper and mix all ingredients in order to blend together.
3. Remove the pan from the heat, leave the contents to cool, stir in the cheese in order to blend with the rest of the ingredients and add some salt if it is needed.
4. Put the flour and salt into a small basin.
5. Open a well in the middle and pour over the water slowly – slowly while kneading in order to make a soft dough that does not stick on hands.
6. Leave the dough covered for one hour and later divide it by forming small balls.
7. Roll the dough, flour it and with the use of a glass cut it into small circles.
8. Place one tea spoon of filling in the middle of each circle and fold it.
9. Press the edges with your fingers and fry the bourekia in hot olive oil until golden on both sides.

INGREDIENTS

FOR THE FILLING

- 1 kilo fennel cut into medium sized pieces
- 2 big onions, finely chopped
- 5 – 6 finely chopped leeks, only the white part
- ½ cup olive oil
- 250 gr grated myzithra cheese
- Salt
- Pepper

FOR THE FILO

- 1 kilo flour for all uses
- Salt
- Lukewarm water for the dough
- Flour for flouring
- Oil for frying

Bourekia with taboura (pumpkin)

INGREDIENTS

FOR THE FILLING

- 1 kilo yellow pumpkin, grated
- 1 big bunch finely chopped fennel
- 3 tbsp finely chopped spearmint
- 2 big onions, finely chopped
- 2 tbsp flour for all uses
- 1 ½ cup grated myzithra cheese
- Salt
- Pepper
- ½ cup olive oil

FOR THE FILO

- 1 kilo flour for all uses
- Salt
- Lukewarm water for the dough
- Oil for frying

PREPARATION

1. Clean, wash and grate the pumpkin.
2. Clean, wash, cut the onions, fennel and spearmint and place them together with the pumpkin into a big pan to sauté them until all cooking liquids evaporate and all ingredients become golden.
3. Remove the pan from the heat and stir in the flour in order to dissolve.
4. Add the cheese and pepper, mix all ingredients in order to blend together, season with salt if that is needed and mix them again.

FOR THE FILO

1. Put the flour and salt into a small basin and mix them.
2. Open a well in the middle and pour over the water slowly while kneading in order to get a soft dough that does not stick on hands.
3. Leave the dough covered for one hour.
4. Divide the dough into medium sized pieces and roll it.
5. Flour the rolled dough and with the use of a glass cut it into small circles.
6. Place in the middle of each circle a tea spoon of filling, fold it and press the edges with your fingers.
7. Fry the bourekia in hot olive oil until golden on both sides.

Pie with yellow pumpkin

INGREDIENTS

- 1 – 1 ½ kilo yellow pumpkin, grated
- ½ kilo grated myzithra cheese
- 5 – 6 finely chopped spring onions
- 3 – 4 finely chopped leeks
- 1 bunch finely chopped fennel
- ½ cup olive oil for the filling
- 4 beaten eggs
- 250 gr grated myzithra cheese
- Salt
- Pepper
- 500 gr ready filo pastry[1] or see the recipe for spinach pie filo
- Some olive oil to brush on the pastry

[1] Pastry rolled in sheets.

PREPARATION

1. Cut the pumpkin, wash and grate it at the grater's side for onion.

2. Season with salt, leave for 15 minutes and squeeze it with your hands to get rid of its juices.

3. Place it into a bowl, add the rest of the ingredients and mix them all until they blend together.

4. Brush olive oil on the surface of a baking tray and lay 3 sheets of filo brushing them one by one with olive oil.

5. Put half of the filling, spread it of filo and lay on top of it 2 more sheets brushed with olive oil.

6. Put the rest of the filling and spread it.

7. Fold the sheets from the sides on top of the filling and cover the pie with 3 sheets brushed with olive oil.

8. Cut the sheets that remain left out of the baking tray, mark the surface in portions, brush olive oil on it and bake the pie at 180ºC degrees for one hour.

Spinach pie

INGREDIENTS

FOR THE FILLING

- 1 kilo finely chopped spinach
- ½ kilo finely chopped kafkalithres and mironia
- 1 bunch finely chopped dill
- 2 big onions, finely chopped
- 300 gr grated myzithra cheese
- 1 cup olive oil
- Salt (optionally)
- Pepper

FOR THE FILO

- 1 kilo flour for all uses
- Some flour for flouring the filo sheets
- Salt
- Oil for brushing the filo sheets
- Lukewarm water as much as needed

PREPARATION

1. Clean the spinach, greens, dill and onions, wash, cut and place them into a big pan to sauté them until most cooking liquids evaporate and they become golden.
2. Remove the pan from the heat, add the pepper, cheese and mix all ingredients until they blend together and some salt if it is needed.
3. Put the flour and salt into a small basin, mix them and open a well in the middle of the dough.
4. Pour over slowly some lukewarm water while kneading in order to get soft dough that does not stick on hands.
5. Leave the dough covered for one hour.
6. Divide the dough into four pieces and roll four sheets.
7. Brush olive oil on the surface of the baking tray and spread the two sheets brushed with olive oil.
8. Add the filling spread it and fold the edges of the filo sheets on top of the filling.
9. Cover the pie with the rest of the sheets, brushed with olive oil one by one and cut the sheets that remain left out of the baking tray.
10. Brush olive oil on the surface of the pie and mark it in portions.
11. Bake it in medium heated oven for 45 minutes – 1 hour until golden.

Tiganopita[1]

PREPARATION

1. Put into a small basin the olive oil, salt, raki and aniseed and mix the ingredients until they blend together.

2. Stir in the flour and pour over the water slowly while kneading in order to make soft dough that does not stick on hands.

3. Roll the dough into filo sheets and cut it in rectangles around 5 x 10 cm.

4. Put olive oil into the frying pan in order to get hot and fry the pies until golden.

5. Place the pies on a platter and sprinkle cheese on them.

INGREDIENTS

- 1 kilo flour
- 1 cup olive oil
- Oil for frying
- 1 espresso cup raki[2]
- 1 tsp salt
- Lukewarm water for the dough
- 300 gr grated myzithra cheese
- 1 tbsp aniseed powder

[1] Fried pie.

[2] Raki or Tsikoudia is a strong distilled spirit containing approximately 37% alcohol per volume and is produced from the must-residue of the wine-press.

Cheese pie

INGREDIENTS

- ¼ kilo grated myzithra cheese
- ¼ kilo fresh kathoura cheese, grated
- 5 beaten eggs
- ½ cup semolina
- 4 cups milk
- 1 cup fresh or dried spearmint, finely chopped
- 10 sheets of filo for pie
- Olive oil for brushing the filo sheets

PREPARATION

1. Put the milk into a pan over low heat, add the semolina, stir until thick, remove from the heat and leave it to cool.

2. Whisk the eggs and add them into the pan.

3. Stir in the cheeses and spearmint and mix all ingredients until they blend together.

4. Brush the surface of a baking tray with olive oil and lay half of the filo sheets brushed with olive oil one by one.

5. Add the filling and spread it.

6. Fold the edges of the filo sheets on top of the filling and cover the pie with the rest of the filo sheets, brushed with olive oil one by one.

7. Cut the sheets that remain left out of the baking tray with a knife or fold the edges of the bottom sheets with the edges of the top sheets forming thus a kind of lace all around.

8. Brush olive oil on the surface of the pie, mark it in portions and bake it in preheated oven at 180°C degrees for 45 minutes.

9. Leave it to cool and cut it.

Pie with greens

INGREDIENTS

- 1 kilo wild greens (kafkalithres, mironia, galatsides), finely chopped
- 1 bunch finely chopped fennel
- 10 finely chopped spring onions
- 4 beaten eggs
- 2 cups grated myzithra cheese
- 1 cup olive oil
- 10 sheets filo for pie
- 1 crumbled rusk
- Pepper
- Salt at the end, if it is needed
- Olive oil for brushing the filo sheets

PREPARATION

1. Clean, wash and chop finely the greens.
2. Put into a big pan the olive oil, greens, spring onions and sauté them while stirring until they become soft and all cooking liquids evaporate.
3. Remove the pan from the heat, leave it to cool and add the fennel, myzithra cheese, eggs, pepper and mix all ingredients until they blend together.
4. Taste the filling and add some salt if that is needed.
5. Lay 5 filo sheets on a baking tray, brushed with olive oil one by one.
6. Add the filling, spread it fold the side filo sheets on top of the filling, cover the pie with the rest of the filo sheets and brushe with olive oil one by one.
7. Cut the filo sheets that remain left out of the baking tray with the use of a knife or fold the edges of the bottom sheets with the edges of the top sheets creating thus a kind of lace all around.
8. Mark the surface in portions, brush it with olive oil and bake it in medium heated oven for 1 hour.

Practical mind and simplicity were the key words even at bread making. Once in a week, the Ikarian housewife was kneading and baking the bread for the week. In Ikarian cuisine there is not a big variety in breads.

Bread and bread varieties

Preparation of sour dough

INGREDIENTS

- 2 cups white flour + 6 tbsp flour
- Salt
- Lukewarm water

PREPARATION

1. Put into a small basin two cups of flour, some salt and mix them together.

2. Add the lukewarm water slowly while kneading in order to get soft dough.

3. Cover the small basin with a towel and leave the dough for 3 days in a warm place until it rises and becomes sour.

4. At the fourth day add three table spoons of flour, pour over little lukewarm water slowly while kneading until get a soft dough, cover with a towel and leave for another three days in a warm place.

5. At the fourth day add three more table spoons of flour and while kneading pour over some lukewarm water until get even softer dough.

6. Cover again the small basin with a towel, leave it for three more days in a warm place and at the fourth day use the sour dough for the preparation of bread.

Bread with sour dough

PREPARATION

1. Dissolve the sour dough with some lukewarm water overnight, add some flour and mix the ingredients in order to get a thick pulp. (Add some more warm water if that is necessary).

2. Cover with towel and leave it overnight.

3. In the morning add the salt, honey, the rest of the flour, knead while pouring over some lukewarm water if it is needed, until get tender dough that does not stick on hands.

4. Form the breads in the shape that want, moisten them little bit with your hands, sprinkle sesame on them, place them on baking trays brushed with olive oil and cover them with towels or something warmer.

5. Leave them to rise while covered with a clean towel in a warm place for 2 – 3 hours.

6. Mark their surface and bake them in medium heated oven for 50 – 60 minutes.

7. Fifteen minutes before take them out of the oven, sprinkle some water on them and leave until baking time is off.

INGREDIENTS

- 1 ½ kilo wheat flour or 1 kilo white flour and 500 gr whole wheat flour
- 1 tbsp salt
- 1 tbsp honey
- 1 ½ cup sour dough
- Lukewarm water for the dough

Country bread

INGREDIENTS

- 1 kilo white flour
- ½ kilo whole wheat or barley flour
- 4 tbsp olive oil
- 60 – 80 gr yeast
- Salt
- Some more white flour
- Some olive oil for the tray

PREPARATION

1. Dissolve the yeast with 2 cups of lukewarm water into a big bowl.

2. Add half of the white flour and mix it with the dissolved yeast until get a thick pulp.

3. Cover it with towels and leave it in a warm place in order to rise. (It should be double in volume and some bubbles should be formed on the surface).

4. When it becomes double, add the olive oil, salt, the rest of the flour and lukewarm water, as much as it is needed in order to get dough that does not stick on our hands.

5. Add some lukerwarm water if it is needed. Knead well all ingredients until get dough that does not stick on hands.

6. Cover the dough with towels and leave it in a warm place to rise for 2 – 3 hours.

7. Form the breads in any shape you want, put them on a baking tray brushed with olive oil in order to rise covered in a warm place for 1 hour.

8. Bake them in preheated oven at 180°C degrees for 40 – 45 minutes.

Brown bread with yeast

INGREDIENTS

- 750 gr whole wheat flour
- 250 gr rye flour
- 50 – 80 gr yeast
- 1 heaped tbsp salt
- 2 tbsp honey
- 4 tbsp oil

PREPARATION

1. Dissolve overnight the yeast with some lukewarm water into a big bowl.
2. Add some whole wheat flour in order to get a thick pulp.
3. Cover the bowl with a towel and leave it to rise until some bubbles are formed on the surface.
4. Put the rest of the whole wheat flour into a basin, add the yeast and knead until get tender dough.
5. Cover the dough with some warm clothes and leave it overnight to rise.
6. In the morning add the rest of the flour, the olive oil, salt, honey and as much lukewarm water as it is needed in order to get soft dough.
7. Knead well all ingredients to get soft dough and form the breads in any shape you want.
8. Place the breads on baking trays, cover them with towels and leave them to rise for one hour.
9. Bake them in preheated oven at 180°C degrees for about one hour.
10. Fifteen minutes before remove them from the oven sprinkle with water and leave them to bake.

Hot bread

PREPARATION

They used to take a small amount from the bread dough and press it with the fingers to form a thin pie.

They were baking it at the oven and they were eating it hot with cheese or olives.

Lagana[1]

INGREDIENTS

- 1 kilo flour
- 50 – 60 gr yeast
- ½ cup olive oil + some olive oil to brush the baking tray
- 2 tbsp honey
- 1 tsp salt
- 1 cup sesame
- Flour for flouring the dough

PREPARATION

1. Dissolve the yeast in a cup of lukewarm water and leave it covered until it becomes double in volume and bubbles are formed on the surface.

2. Put the flour, salt, honey and olive oil into a basin and mix them together.

3. Add the yeast and knead until get a soft dough that does not stick on hands.

4. Cover the dough with towels and a blanket and leave it in a warm place to become double in volume.

5. Divide the dough in pieces at the size of a big apple, flour them slightly and roll them with the rolling pin in oval shape 1 cm thick.

6. Make shallow wells with your fingers on the surface of lagana.

7. With wet fingers or with a brush moisten the surface of lagana and sprinkle sesame on it.

8. Place them on a baking tray brushed with olive oil and bake them in preheated oven at 180°C degrees until they get golden.

[1] A type of bread.

Lazarakia[1] for easter

INGREDIENTS

- The same ingredients used for the preparation of bread with the addition of eggs and herbs like mastic, aniseed, cloves, sesame and mavrokouki.

PREPARATION

1. Prepare the dough according to the recipe for bread.

2. Add 1 tbsp mastic and knead in order that all ingredients blend together.

3. Divide the dough in pieces at the shape of orange and roll them like thick laces.

4. Form braids from the laces, brush them with egg, sprinkle them with mavrokouki and place a red egg on top of them.

5. Place them on a baking tray, brushed with olive oil and bake them in preheated oven at 180°C until they get golden.

[1] A special type of bread eaten during Easter. Mawrokouki black sesame.

Litpurgia (prosforo)[1]

INGREDIENTS

- ½ kilo white flour
- Lukewarm water, as much as needed for forming a tighter dough
- ½ cup sour dough
- 1 tsp aniseed
- Salt

[1] A type of bread prepared as an offering to the church for the ritual of Holy Communion.

PREPARATION

1. Put the flour into a basin, add the aniseed and mix them well.
2. Make a well in the centre and add the sour dough dissolved in ½ cup lukewarm water and the salt, knead and add some more lukewarm water in order to get tighter dough that does not stick on hands.
3. Cover the dough with towels and leave it in a warm place to become double volume (to rise).
4. When it rises knead it again and form a round loaf.
5. Press at the centre the special stamp with the cross and cover it again to rise for about one hour.
6. Bake in medium heated oven, preheated, for 50 – 60 minutes.

Lipsopites

INGREDIENTS

- 1 kilo flour
- ½ cup olive oil
- 1 tsp salt
- Water as much as needed for the making of tighter dough
- Some olive oil for brushing the frying pan

PREPARATION

1. Put the flour and salt into a basin and mix them together.
2. Add the olive oil and while kneading pour over the water until get tight dough.
3. Leave the dough covered for one hour.
4. Divide the dough into small balls and spread them with the palm of your hand until they become like souvlaki pita (half centimeter thick, round at the size of a fruit plate).
5. Place the frying pan over the heat to become hot.
6. Brush olive oil the frying pan and fry them until golden on both sides.

When the bread was finished and there was not enough time to prepare new bread, they were making a quick bread, lipsopita. Lipsopites resemble to souvlaki pita (pie).

Barley rusks

INGREDIENTS

- 1 kilo whole barley flour
- ½ kilo white flour
- 60 gr yeast
- 1 cup olive oil
- 2 tsp aniseed
- 3 -4 tbsp raki
- 1 tbsp salt
- White flour for the kneading

PREPARATION

1. Put into large bowl 2 cups lukewarm water and dissolve the yeast.
2. Add half of the white flour, mix them until get a pulp, cover it with towels, leave it in a warm place to rise and become double.
3. Put the rest of the flour, aniseed and salt into a basin, mix them and form a well at the centre.
4. Add the olive oil, raki and yeast and knead while pouring over the lukewarm water slowly until get homogeneous dough that does not stick on the basin.
5. Cover the dough with towels and leave it in a warm place for one and a half hour to become double. (If the environment is cold also cover it with a blanket).
6. Put the dough into another basin, flour it and knead for another 5 minutes.
7. Take pieces from the dough and form small roills.
8. Mark slices on the small roills, place them on a baking tray brushed with olive oil, cover them with a towel and leave them in a warm place to rise, for one hour.
9. Preheat the oven at 180°C to 200°C and bake them for one hour.
10. Remove them from the oven and leave them to cool.
11. Cut them into slices, place them on the baking tray and leave them to dry in the oven at 50°C for 3–4 hours.

Hristopsomo
(bread of Jesus)

INGREDIENTS

- Follow the recipe for making bread, add some aniseed or crushed cloves, some crushed walnuts and knead all ingredients to blend together.

PREPARATION

Form a loaf and knead the dough into two laces at the thickness of a finger which use in order to create a cross that place on top of the loaf. Put a walnut at the centre, sprinkle with sesame and bake them in the same way as the bread.

Sweets

Amigdalota[1]

INGREDIENTS

- 500 gr almonds
- 250 gr sugar
- 1 cup water
- ½ tsp crushed mastic
- 2 sachets vanilla powder
- 300 gr caster sugar
- Cloves to garnish

PREPARATION

1. Put the almonds into a pan with boiling water and bring them to the boil a few times until their skin becomes soft.
2. Drain the almonds, leave them to cool and rub them with a towel in order to remove their skin.
3. Beat them inside a mortar until they melt and place them into a basin.
4. Put the sugar into a small pan and boil it with water until syrup is formed. Leave it to cool.
5. In the basin with the almonds add the mastic, vanilla and slowly the syrup, kneading all ingredients until they become a dough medium tight.
6. Divide the dough into small pieces at the size of a walnut, press it at one side with your three hand fingers and form small pears.
7. Coat them with caster sugar and place at their top a clove.

[1] Almond sweets.

Amigdalota in the oven

PREPARATION

1. Boil for two minutes the almonds to soak their skin, remove the skin and spread them on a towel.
2. Beat them in the mortar or in blender in order to melt and place them into a basin.
3. Add the egg whites beaten into a tight meringue, the sugar, lemon zest and juice, brandy, mastic, add slowly – slowly the rusk and mix all ingredients with your hand in order to blend together.
4. The dough should be medium tight.
5. If the dough is too tight, add some lemon juice or brandy.
6. If the dough is waterish add some crumbled rusk.
7. Roll the dough into pieces at the thickness of a finger or in round shape.
8. Spread some waxed paper on the baking tray and place the amigdalota on top of it.
9. Bake them in preheated oven at 180°C for 15–20 minutes.
10. Remove them from the oven and sprinkle them with rosewater.
11. Leave them to cool, coat them in caster sugar and place a clove on top of each one.

INGREDIENTS

- 700 gr almonds
- 5 egg whites, tight meringue
- 1 cup sugar
- 1 cup crumbled white rusk or toasted bread
- Grated zest of 2 lemons and their juice
- 1 tsp crushed mastic
- ¼ cup brandy
- 1 tbsp crushed cloves

FOR SPRINKLING AND COATING

- 1 kilo caster sugar
- Rosewater
- Cloves for decoration

Sweet pumpkin pie (tabouras)

INGREDIENTS

- 1 kilo grated yellow pumpkin
- 2 cups crushed walnuts
- 1 cup raisins without seeds
- 1 cup honey
- 1 cup crumbled rusk or toasted bread
- 3 tbsp grated cinnamon
- ½ cup olive oil
- Olive oil for brushing the filo sheets
- Cinnamon for sprinkling

FOR THE FILO SHEETS DOUGH

- 1 kilo flour for all uses
- ½ cup olive oil
- ½ tsp salt
- Water as much as needed for the making of medium tight dough that does not stick on our hands
- Flour for flouring the filo sheets

1. Clean the pumpkin, wash, grate, squeeze it with your hands in order to lose its liquids and leave it into the colander for 2 – 3 hours.
2. Squeeze again the pumpkin to extract its liquids and place it into a basin.
3. Add the crushed walnuts, crumbled rusk, raisins, olive oil, honey, cinnamon and sugar and mix all ingredients in order to blend together.
4. Put the flour and salt into a basin and mix them together.
5. Stir in the olive oil.
6. Pour over the water slowly and knead until get tight dough that does not stick on hands.
7. Leave the dough covered for 20 – 30 minutes.
8. Roll 4 filo sheets.
9. Brush a baking tray with olive oil and spread the two brushed filo with olive oil one by one.
10. Add the filling and spread it.
11. Cover the rest of the filo sheets one by one after being brushed with olive oil.
12. Fold tightly the edges of the bottom filo sheets over the edges of the top filo sheets creating thus a kind of a lace all around the baking tray and mark the surface in portions.

13. Bake the pie in preheated oven at 180°C for almost one hour.

14. Leave the pie to cool and sprinkle cinnamon on its surface.

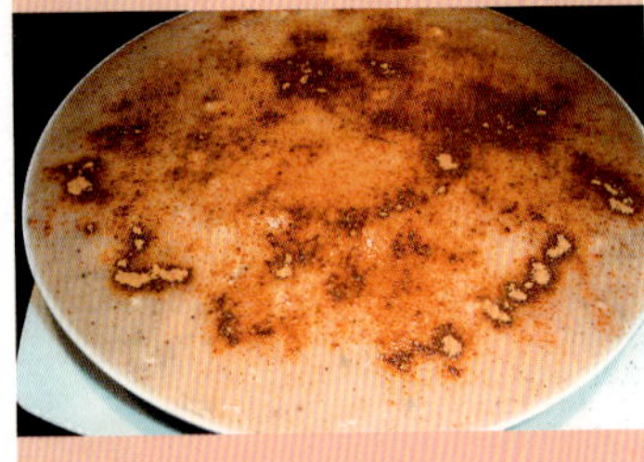

Cream of kolivozoumo (pulp)

INGREDIENTS

- 1 cup flour
- ½ cup crushed walnuts
- 3 tbsp grated cinnamon
- ½ cup sugar
- 5 cups wheat stock
- ½ cup boiled wheat

PREPARATION

1. Put the wheat stock into a pan and dissolve the flour into it.
2. Add the sugar, wheat, one tbsp cinnamon, the crushed walnuts and stir all ingredients until the cream becomes thick.
3. Serve in small bowls, leave it to cool and sprinkle them with cinnamon.

When the housewives were boiling wheat in order to make koliva[1], they were keeping the wheat stock and with some boiled wheat they were preparing a cream.

[1] A type of sweet made of wheat offered at every funeral memorials.

Kourabiedes[1]

INGREDIENTS

- ½ kilo milk butter
- 1 cup sugar
- 2 whole eggs and 2 egg yolks
- 1 small cup brandy
- 1 tbsp baking powder
- 3 vanilla sachets
- 1/2 kilo almonds, roasted and crushed
- Soft flour as much as needed in order to get soft dough that does not stick on hands when roll it
- ½ kilo caster sugar
- ½ cup rosewater

PREPARATION

1. Put the butter into a basin and beat it strongly for 5 minutes.
2. Add the eggs and the egg yolks, vanilla, brandy and sugar and beat all ingredients strongly until the sugar melts and until they blend together.
3. Stir in the almonds and baking powder mixed with a cup of flour.
4. Mix all ingredients in order to blend together and add slowly the flour while kneading in order to get soft dough.
5. Roll the kourabiedes in round shapes or in the shape of half – moon and place them on a baking tray brushed with butter.
6. Bake them in preheated oven at 180°C for 25 – 30 minutes.
7. Remove them from the oven and leave them to cool.
8. Place them on a platter and sprinkle them with rosewater and caster sugar.

[1] A type of Greek almond shortbread offered during Christmas.

Loukoumades

INGREDIENTS

FOR THE DOUGH

- 500 gr flour for all uses
- 50 gr yeast
- 2 tsp sugar
- 1 tsp salt
- Water as much as needed in order to get a thick pulp
- Olive oil for frying

FOR THE SYRUP

- 3 ½ cups honey
- 1 ½ cup water
- 2 cinnamon sticks

FOR THE GARNISH

- 1 cup crumbled walnuts
- Grated cinnamon

PREPARATION

SYRUP

1. Put into a pan the water, honey and cinnamon sticks and leave them to boil.

2. Mix all ingredients until they blend together and bring them to the boil for 2 – 3 times, skim off the foam and leave the syrup to cool.

LOUKOUMADES´ DOUGH

3. Dissolve the yeast into a bowl with soma lukewarm water.

4. Add 4 table spoons flour and the sugar.

5. Mix the ingredients in order to dissolve and until get a pulp.

6. Leave it in a warm place for 20 – 30 minutes until some bubbles appear on the surface.

7. Put the flour and salt into a basin and mix them in order to blend together. Open a well in the centre.

8. Add the yeast mixture and slowly – slowly some lukewarm water while stirring in order to get a homogeneous thick pulp.

9. Put the olive oil into a deep pan so that the loukoumades will “dive” into it.

10. With the use of a tea spoon that dip in the water constantly, take a small tea spoon of the pulp each time and “dive” it into the hot olive oil.

11. Leave the loukoumades to become slightly golden and remove them from the olive oil with a slotted spoon.

12. Place them on a platter with some kitchen paper in order to drain olive oil.

13. Remove the kitchen paper from the platter, pour the syrup over loukoumades and sprinkle them with walnuts and cinnamon.

Moustalevria

(must-jelly)

INGREDIENTS

- 10 cups boiled and strained must
- 2 cups flour
- 1 ½ cup crushed walnuts
- ½ cup roasted sesame
- 3 tbsp grated cinnamon
- If the must is not boiled, need pure ashes from wood in order to boil it, skim off the foam and strain it.

BOILING OF MUST

1. Put 11 – 12 cups of must into a pan with 2 cups of ashes which have closed it into a tight bag made of voile.
2. Leave it to boil for 30 minutes skimming off the foam.
3. Remove the pan from the heat, discard the voile with the ashes and leave the must for 4 – 5 hours to stand.
4. Strain it through a colander and with the use of voile and use the must for the moustalevria.

PREPARATION OF MOUSTALEVRIA

1. Dissolve the flour into little bit of must
2. Put the rest of the must into a pan and place it over the heat.
3. As soon as it becomes warm add the flour, mix in order to be completely dissolved, reduce the heat and leave the mixture to stand while stirring constantly to avoid the creation of any lumps.
4. As soon as it stands, place it into small bowls which and sprinkle it with cinnamon, sesame and walnuts.
5. Leave it to cool and serve.

Baklava

INGREDIENTS

- 12 filo sheets
- 300 gr crushed walnuts
- 200 gr crushed almonds
- 1 cup sesame
- 2 tbsp grated cinnamon
- 4 heaped tbsp honey
- Olive oil for brushing the filo sheets
- Cloves for decoration

FOR THE SYRUP

- 2 ½ cups honey
- 2 cups sugar
- 2 ½ cups water
- 2 – 3 cinnamon sticks
- 1 tbsp cloves
- 2 tbsp lemon juice

PREPARATION

1. Mix the crushed walnuts, crushed almonds, sesame, honey and cinnamon into a small basin.
2. Brush olive oil on a baking tray and lay 4 filo sheets one by one after brush them with olive oil.
3. Spread some filling on them and cover with 2 filo sheets brushed with olive oil one by one.
4. Spread some more of the filling and cover with 2 filo sheets brushed with olive oil.
5. Spread the rest of the filling and fold the filo sheets that remain left out of the baking tray on top of the filling.
6. Cover with 4 filo sheets brushed with olive oil one by one and cut the sheets that remain left out of the baking tray.
7. Mark deeply the baklava into portions, put a clove on each portion and bake in preheated oven at 180°C until golden.
8. Boil the ingredients for the syrup for 5 – 10 minutes, remove the cinnamon and cloves with a slotted spoon and throw them away.
9. Pour the syrup over the baked baklava, allow it to be absorbed and wait for baklava to cool.
10. Cut the baklava, place it on a platter and serve.

Xerotigana

INGREDIENTS

- 600 gr flour in order to get tight dough which it can be rolled without sticking on our fingers
- 5 eggs
- 1/2 cup ouzo or raki
- 2 tbsp olive oil
- ½ tsp crated mastic
- ½ tsp soda powder
- 1 heaped tbsp sugar
- ½ tsp salt
- Olive oil for frying

FOR THE SYRUP

- 3 ½ cups honey
- 1 ½ cup water
- 1 tbsp cloves
- 2 cinnamon sticks

FOR SPRINKLING

- 1 cup crushed walnuts
- ½ cup roasted sesame

PREPARATION

1. Put the eggs, ouzo, soda, mastic, olive oil, sugar and salt into a basin and whisk them until they blend together.
2. Stir in the flour slowly while kneading in order to get tight dough that does not stick on your hands.
3. Leave the dough covered with a towel for 30 minutes.
4. Divide the dough into pieces at the size of an orange and roll each piece into a thin filo sheet.
5. With the special utensil cut the filo sheets into strips 5 X 8 cm and press them with your fingers at the centre creating thus small bows.
6. Place them into a frying pan with hot olive oil and fry them on both sides until slightly golden.
7. Remove them from the frying pan with a slotted spoon and place them on a tray with kitchen paper for one hour in order to drain.
8. Discard the kitchen paper and place the xerotigana on a platter in order to cool.
9. Put the ingredients for the syrup into a pan, boil them for 5 – 10 minutes and remove the syrup from the heat.

10. With the use of a slotted spoon dip the xerotigana into the syrup for one minute, place them on a clean platter and sprinkle them with crushed walnuts and roasted sesame.

Tiganites (pancakes)

INGREDIENTS

- ½ kilo flour
- ½ tsp salt
- Olive oil for frying
- Grape – juice syrup (petimezi) or honey or sugar
- Cinnamon

PREPARATION

1. Put the flour into a small basin and add the salt, mix them together and pour over the water slowly until get a medium (thick) pulp.

2. Leave the pulp inside the small basin for 30 minutes and stir it for 2 – 3 minutes.

3. Put enough olive oil into a frying pan in order to become hot and with the use of a spoon put the pulp into the frying pan creating thus the pancakes.

4. Leave them until golden on both sides, place them on a platter with kitchen paper in order to drain, remove the kitchen paper and pour over the pancakes grape – juice syrup or honey, or sprinkle them with sugar and grated cinnamon.

5. Serve them hot.

Finikia (recipe No 1)

INGREDIENTS

- 3 cups olive oil
- 2 cups sugar
- ½ cup orange juice
- Grated zest of an orange
- Grated zest of one lemon
- 2 tbsp crushed cloves
- 1 tbsp grated cinnamon
- 1 glass aloussa or 1 glass beer
- 1 tsp soda
- Flour as much as needed in order to get soft dough that does not stick on hands

PREPARATION

1. Boil 1 ½ glass of water into a small pan.

2. Add 4 table spoons ashes from clean wood, closed into a voile bag.

3. Bring them to the boil, discard the voile bag with the ashes and keep the water aside for 4 – 5 hours in order to allow the ashes to stay at the bottom of the small pan.

4. Strain the water while being careful not to spill the ashes inside the clean glass.

5. Put the olive oil, sugar, aloussa (the water boiled with the ashes), zests of orange and lemon, cinnamon, cloves, the soda dissolved in the orange juice and whisk all ingredients very well in order to blend together.

6. Stir in the flour slowly – slowly until get soft dough that does not stick on hands when roll it.

7. Roll the finikia into round or oval (like madelein) shapes, press them on top with the cheese grater creating

different designs on them and bake them on a baking tray brushed with olive oil in preheated oven at 180ºC for 20 – 25 minutes.

8. Remove them from the oven and allow them to cool.

9. Put the ingredients for the syrup into a pan and leave them to boil for 10 minutes.

10. With the use of a slotted spoon dip the finikia into the syrup for 1 – 2 minutes and place them afterwards on a platter.

11. Sprinkle them with the crushed walnuts and leave them to cool.

12. If do not dip them in syrup, mix the sugar with the cinnamon and sprinkle the finikia with this mixture.

INGREDIENTS

FOR THE SYRUP

- 2 ½ cups honey
- 2 cups sugar
- 2 ½ cups water
- 2 cinnamon sticks

FOR SPRINKLING

- 2 cups crushed walnuts
- If you do not want to use syrup, mix ½ kilo of sugar with 4 table spoons of grated cinnamon and sprinkle this mixture on the finikia.

Finikia (recipe No 2)

INGREDIENTS

- 4 glasses (approximately) soft flour or as much as needed in order to get soft dough that does not stick on hands when roll it
- 1 glass olive oil
- ½ glass orange juice
- Grated zests of one orange and one lemon
- ½ glass aloussa (water with ashes) or ½ tbsp soda
- ½ glass brandy
- 1 tsp baking powder
- 1 tbsp crushed cloves
- 1 tbsp grated cinnamon
- ½ glass sugar
- 2 glasses crushed walnuts for sprinkling

PREPARATION

1. Put 1 ½ glass of water into a small pan and place it over the heat.
2. Add ashes from clean wood closed into a bag made of voile and bring them to the boil for a couple of times.
3. Remove the small pan from the heat, discard the voile bag with the ashes and wait until the ashes left in the water stay at the bottom of the pan.
4. Strain the water with the use of some clean voile and keep ½ glass of it for the finikia.
5. Put the olive oil, water with ashes, orange juice, brandy and sugar into a basin and whisk them until the sugar dissolves and all ingredients blend together.
6. Stir in the grated zests of orange and lemon, the cloves, one table spoon of cinnamon, and the baking powder until they blend together with the rest of the ingredients.
7. Stir in the flour slowly while kneading in order to get soft dough that does not stick on hands when roll it.

8. Roll the finikia into round or oval (like madelein) shapes.

9. Press gently the cheese grater at the top of the finikia creating thus different designs and place them on baking trays brushed with olive oil.

10. Bake them in preheated oven at 180°C for 20 – 25 minutes and leave them to cool.

11. Put the ingredients for the syrup into a pan, bring them to the boil for 2 – 3 times and remove the pan from the heat.

12. With the use of a slotted spoon, dip the finikia into the syrup for 1 – 2 minutes and place them afterwards on a platter.

13. Sprinkle with crushed walnuts and leave them to cool.

14. If do not want to use syrup, mix the sugar with the cinnamon and sprinkle the finikia with this mixture.

INGREDIENTS

FOR THE SYRUP

- 2 ½ cups honey
- 2 cups sugar
- 2 ½ cups water
- 2 cinnamon sticks
- If you do not want to use syrup, mix 1 glass of sugar with 2 – 3 table spoons grated cinnamon and sprinkle the finikia with this mixture.

Halva

INGREDIENTS

- 2 cups semolina
- 1 cup olive oil
- 1 cup coarsely crushed almonds
- ½ cup raisins (without seeds)

FOR THE SYRUP

- ½ cup honey
- 2 cups sugar
- Zest of one lemon
- 1 tsp cloves
- 2 cinnamon sticks and 1 tbsp grated cinnamon
- 5 cups water

FOR SPRINKLING

- Cinnamon
- 15 whole almonds without the skin

PREPARATION

1. Put all the ingredients for the syrup into a pan and boil them for 5 minutes.

2. Discard all spices with a slotted spoon and keep the syrup aside.

3. Put the semolina and the crushed almonds into a pan over low heat and stir them constantly until they get slightly golden and later add the olive oil.

4. Mix and sauté the ingredients with the olive oil and remove them from the heat.

5. Add the raisins while stirring until all ingredients blend together and pour over the syrup while constantly stirring.

6. Put the pan over low heat while stirring and bring it to the boil until halva sets.

7. Place halva into a mould and it becomes cool turn it over on a platter.

8. Sprinkle with cinnamon and decorate with almonds.

Fruit conserves

Sour cherry

INGREDIENTS

- 1 kilo sour cherries
- 1 ½ kilo sugar
- 2 – 3 tbsp lemon juice
- 1 cup water
- 1 bunch apple geranium or 2 vanilla sachets

PREPARATION

1. Wash the sour cherries, remove the stems and with a special utensil discard the seeds without melting the fruits.

2. Put the sour cherries, sugar and water into a pan and leave them to drain their juices for 4 – 5 hours.

3. Boil the ingredients for 10 minutes and with the use of a slotted spoon skim off the foam.

4. Add the apple geranium and the lemon juice.

5. Leave the sweet to set and remove it from the heat.

6. Discard the apple geranium and with the use of a slotted spoon remove the sour cherries and put them into jars while put their syrup into bottles to be used as a sour cherry beverage.

Quince

INGREDIENTS

- 1 kilo finely chopped quinces
- 1 kilo sugar
- 2 – 3 tbsp lemon juice
- 2/3 cup almonds without the skin
- 1 bunch apple geranium or 2 sachets vanilla
- 1 ½ cup water

PREPARATION

1. Peel the skin of the quinces, quarter them and discard the tough parts and the seeds.

2. Wash and cut them into thin slices.

3. Place the quinces into a pan with the water, cover and leave them to boil until softened but not melted.

4. Add the sugar and place them over high temperature heat in order to boil.

5. Stir in the apple geranium and almonds and when the sweet begins to set, add the lemon juice.

6. When it sets leave it to cool, discard the apple geranium and store the sweet into jars.

Sour orange

INGREDIENTS

- 1 kilo green sour oranges at the same size
- 1 ½ kilo sugar
- Juice of one lemon
- 2 cups water
- 2 – 3 cinnamon sticks

PREPARATION

1. Grate gently the sour oranges in order to remove the green part of their skin and with a special utensil or a sharp small knife open a hole in the centre and remove their seeds.
2. Wash the sour oranges and boil them into plenty of water until softened.
3. Discard the water where they were boiled and place them into plenty of cold water for 2 days while changing it every 4 – 5 hours in order to lose any bitterness in taste and afterwards drain them.
4. Put the water, sugar and cinnamon into a pan and bring them to the boil for a few times while skimming off the foam.
5. Add the sour oranges, bring them to the boil 5 – 6 times and remove the pan from the heat.
6. Leave them covered for 15 hours.
7. Add the lemon juice and boil them until they set.
8. Leave the sweet to cool and store it into jars.

Sour orange (skins)

INGREDIENTS

- 40 skins of sour oranges
- 1 ½ kilo sugar
- 4 cups water
- 3 tbsp lemon juice for the syrup
- Juice of 3 lemons

PREPARATION

1. Wash the sour oranges, wipe the water on them and grate the yellow part of their skin in order to remove it.
2. Carve 5 – 6 slices on the skins of the sour oranges, remove the skins, fold them into rolls and with the use of a needle hang them on a strong white thread (10 on each thread) and tie the ends of the strings.
3. Place them into a pan with plenty of boiling water and boil them for 5 minutes.
4. Drain and put them again into plenty of water to boil until softened.
5. Drain and put them into plenty of cold water together with the juice of one lemon and leave them like this in order to lose any bitterness in their taste.
6. Leave the sour oranges in the water for 8 – 10 hours.
7. Every 8 – 10 hours change the water for two more times and each time add the juice of one lemon.
8. Drain the sour oranges and remove them from the thread.
9. Put the water, sugar and table spoon of lemon juice into a pan.
10. Bring to the boil for 3 – 4 times.
11. Take the sour oranges one by one, roll them tightly and put them into the pan with the syrup.

12. Bring them to the boil for 3 – 4 times and remove them from the heat.

13. Cover the pan and leave them inside it for 10 – 15 hours.

14. Place again the pan over the heat, add the rest of the lemon juice and wait for the sweet to set while boiling over high temperature heat.

15. Leave the sweet to cool and store it into glass jars.

Cardinal grape

INGREDIENTS

- 1 kilo cardinal grapes without the skin
- 1 kilo sugar
- 3 – 4 tbsp lemon juice
- 1 bunch apple geranium or 2 vanilla sachets
- 1 cups almonds without the skin
- 1 cup water

PREPARATION

1. Remove the grapes from the stems and make sure that they are not rotten or melted.
2. Wash the grapes, peel their skin and with a special utensil remove their seeds.
3. Put half of the grapes into a pan, form a layer and cover them with half of the sugar.
4. Arrange the rest of the grapes on top of the sugar and top them with the rest of the sugar.
5. Leave the pan covered and allow the grapes to extract their juices for 5 hours.
6. Add the water, almonds and apple geranium and boil all the ingredients over high temperature heat in order that the sweet begins to set.
7. Stir in the lemon juice and leave the sweet to set.
8. Make sure that the sweet will not be spilled from the pan while boiling.
9. Discard the apple geranium, leave the sweet to set and store it into glass jars.

Rose

INGREDIENTS

- 500 gr petals from roses that bloom in April (wild ones with pink flowers)
- 1 kilo sugar
- 3 tbsp lemon juice
- 1 vanilla sachets (optionally)
- ½ tsp citric acid
- ½ cup almonds without the skin

PREPARATION

1. Put the rose petals into a colander and wash them.
2. Put the petals into a pan together with 3 glasses of water and bring them to the boil.
3. Add the vanilla, almonds and sugar and mix all the ingredients until the sugar dissolves and they all blend together.
4. Increase the heat and add the citric acid.
5. When the sweet begins to set add the lemon juice, mix all ingredients and leave the sweet to set.
6. Remove it from the heat, allow it to cool and store it into jars.

Glossary

Aloussa	A dressing of water and ashes
English powder	Baking powder
Galatsida	Wild greens known since antiquity as galaktitis
Glina	A type of "butter" prepared after the processing of pork fat
Glistrida	Wild greens
Kafkalithres	Wild aromatic greens
Karifilia	Clove
Karivoli	Snails
Karonos	The bud of onion
Kathoura	Fresh white cheese made by the milk of goats and sheeps
Kolokasi	Wild potato
Loubinoi	Loubinia[1]
Manites	Mushrooms
Maxouli	The gathered products, the crop
Ovries	A kind of wild greens
Raska	Free range goats
Stifno	Wild greens
Tambouras	Pumpkin
Throubi	Wild herb, tastes and smells like oregano
Tsifia	Dried vegetables
Volvoi	Wild bulbs (wild onions)
Vriha	Fern
Xylangouro	Kind of cucumber (green melon)

[1] Dried seeds that look like dried beans.